Chapter 1. Small Town

The morning was cold, and the colors seemed duller than usual. Something felt off, as if entropy had decided to play with this corner of the world, scattering small bits of chaos everywhere. But let's not dwell on that. We're in a European town—touristic, buried under snow for eight months of the year. From the outside, everything seemed perfect: picturesque streets, pristine facades, and fresh air that some would pay to breathe. But there was something money couldn't buy. This place lacked a soul.

Brooke crossed the street slowly and looked toward the same café as always. Rustic and somewhat depressing to the eye, with fogged-up windows and a crooked “open” sign. It wasn’t particularly inviting, yet something kept her coming back every morning before work. Maybe it was the routine, that automatic mechanism that keeps you going when nothing else does.

As she pushed the door open, the bell jingled in the still air of the café. Mary, the waitress, was wiping down one of the tables with a dingy gray cloth.

“Morning, Brooke. The usual?” she asked with a smile that felt more like a reflex than genuine emotion.

"Yeah, the usual," Brooke replied, not bothering to look up.

She slumped into the last table by the window. From there, she watched as the snow began to fall with an almost irritating calm. She stared outside, lost in thoughts that seemed to spin endlessly in circles. Nothing changes here. Not today, not tomorrow. Maybe next year something new will happen, something that inspires me to try harder. But why bother? I don't expect anything anymore. Nothing can disappoint me now.

"Here's your coffee!" Mary shouted from the counter, but Brooke didn't even flinch.

The waitress walked over to her table, leaning on the back of a chair.

“Hey, Brooke, can you at least pretend to react? Just looking at you brings me down. And believe me, I’ve got enough of that with this crappy job.”

Brooke shook her head as if waking from a dream.
“Right. I’ve got to go; I’m running late.”

She grabbed her coffee and left without another word. The bell jingled again as the door closed behind her, leaving the same place as always, frozen in time.

Her job was at a modest spa—busy, functional on its best days. Brooke arrived at work at exactly 8 a.m., as she always did, not a minute late. Her routine was almost mechanical: hang her coat on the rack, put on her name tag—slightly faded in the top-right corner—and sit behind the desk, ready to greet the few clients who would show up that morning.

"Another day in paradise," she muttered sarcastically as she powered on the old, sluggish monitor used to check appointments.

The place was dull, at least for its employees, but it had its perks. No one demanded too much from her, and as long as she completed her hours, she could spend the rest of her time lost in her own head. It wasn't a bad deal. Enough to pay rent and afford an occasional treat—a fancy coffee here, a used book there. But not much else.

The monotony of the day was broken when Clara, the manager, showed up—a woman in her forties who always seemed on the verge of exhaustion. She entered the spa with an odd look on her face, somewhere between excitement and worry.

“Listen up, everyone, I have an important announcement,” she said, settling at the reception desk. Brooke barely lifted her gaze, just enough to feign interest.

“The spa is changing ownership. A large company has bought it and will turn it into part of their tourist resort. This could be a good thing for all of us."

Brooke nodded indifferently, but in her mind, she couldn't care less.
"So what? Probably the only change will be the logo on the invoices," she thought, turning her focus back to the screen.

Something slightly out of the ordinary happened around noon. A regular client, Mrs. Müller, an elderly woman with unusual energy for her seventy years, arrived for her weekly massage. While waiting for her turn, she began speaking to Brooke from the reception sofa.

"You know, dear, last night I dreamed of black snow. The whole town was covered in it. Isn't that strange? Black as coal. Do you believe in premonitory dreams?"

Brooke simply shook her head, but the image stayed with her. Black snow. There was something oddly unsettling about it, though she decided not to dwell on it.

The rest of the day passed without further incidents. The same clients, the same shallow conversations, the same pointless emails no one read. In the afternoon, Clara offered her a lackluster compliment.

"Brooke, at least you're reliable. That's more than I can say for some."

That's it? That's my achievement? Not skipping work at a place I barely care about. Brooke gave a polite smile, but inside, even the compliments felt dull, empty, like everything else in her life.

At the end of her shift, she put on her coat and stepped out into the cold street. The snow was still falling softly, covering the sidewalks in a white blanket. She stood there for a moment, thinking about what Mrs. Müller had said.

Black as coal. Strange...

Brooke took a deep breath. Another day had ended. And although nothing significant had happened, something inside her felt that, somehow, everything was about to change.

The clock struck 5:00 p.m., and the week's routine had come to an end. The exhaustion from work weighed on every muscle in her body, but Friday always brought the promise of rest. The week had been heavy, but now she had the whole weekend to relax—or so she thought, until a sudden memory interrupted her attempt to unwind.

"Oh, crap... the guys!" she suddenly remembered. Beatriz and Joseph had invited her to a bar that night. The only bar in town, but somehow a place where they always ended up having fun. The memory hit her like a tidal wave, and guilt over forgetting the plan immediately set in. In her mind, the reasons not to go were plenty, but she felt pressured to attend, as always. A sigh escaped her lips, resigned. Well, I hope it's at least fun.

The bar was modest but had the basics: a few pool tables, dice for a quick game, and a slightly run-down atmosphere that somehow gave it a cozy charm. When she walked in, she spotted her friends, who always seemed so cheerful with their lives. She couldn't help but wonder if maybe the problem was her. That something inside her was falling apart, and she didn't know how to stop it.

"Hey! How've you been? It's been ages since I last saw you, gorgeous!" Beatriz greeted her with a beaming smile, hugging her tightly.

"Well, you know... home to work, work to home," Brooke replied with a faint smile. No energy for anything else, she thought to herself as she sat with them.

Joseph, ever the optimist, gave her a concerned look. "But you're only 23! You've got to be doing more than that. Life isn't just work—there's so much out there to do!"

"Yea—," she began, her tone flatter than ever, her gaze lost in the distance as her mind wandered elsewhere. She knew she couldn't afford to do more. Life was slipping through her fingers, and nothing she did seemed to bring her any real joy.

Then, Beatriz, with a grin from ear to ear, shared her news. "I have something amazing to tell you! I got a scholarship to study at one of the top universities in North America. It's a dream come true!"

Both friends surrounded her, congratulating her and celebrating her achievement. Joseph hugged her, his face reflecting genuine pride. And while Brooke felt happy for her friend, she couldn't stop the pang of sadness that ran through her. When will I have something like that? she thought, forcing a smile onto her face.

Before she could process her emotions, Joseph dropped his own announcement. “I’m leaving too... to New Zealand. A job came up there, and I want to try something new.”

Beatriz jumped with joy, hugging him and congratulating him enthusiastically. But Brooke couldn’t take it anymore. Something inside her broke. Her friends’ warmth, their smiles, everything that seemed perfect for them only highlighted how insignificant she felt. She sat there, frozen, staring at her hands, unable to hide the lump in her throat.

“Brooke... what’s wrong?” Beatriz asked, noticing her shift in demeanor.

With a broken expression, Brooke tried to smile, but tears began streaming down her face uncontrollably. "It's just that... it makes me sad knowing that in a few months, I won't see you both as often. You're both getting everything you've ever wanted, and I... I'm staying here with nothing."

Joseph and Beatriz didn't fully understand the depth of her pain, but their expressions softened. Why can't I just be happy for them? Brooke wondered as she tried to calm herself. It wasn't their fault she didn't know how to break free from the rut she was trapped in. But what truly tore her apart was the idea of losing her two closest friends—the only ones she had left.

After a few moments of silence, Beatriz hugged her. “Hey, everything’s going to be okay. We’re not saying goodbye, just ‘see you later.’ We’ll keep in touch, alright?”

Brooke nodded, wiping away her tears. “You’re right. I shouldn’t be so dramatic,” she said with a half-smile, her voice still trembling.

Joseph raised his beer. “Alright, enough with the sadness, yeah? Let’s celebrate.”

And so they did. The night went on with laughter, rounds of pool, dice games, and conversations that, for a little while, lifted the weight from her shoulders.

The evening was in full swing when Erick, one of Brooke's coworkers, walked in with a guy she didn't recognize right away. The newcomer seemed slightly out of place.

"Brooke! What's up? What are you doing here?" Erick greeted her enthusiastically, as if the night had just gotten more exciting.

"Just hanging out with some friends I haven't seen in a while," Brooke replied, smiling as her gaze shifted to the new guy, who seemed a bit uncomfortable in the setting.

"This is Leo," Erick said. "He's been around for a few months. He's working at the same resort as us, saving up some money."

"Nice to meet you," Brooke said with a polite smile, extending her hand toward Leo.

"Nice to meet you," Leo replied, shaking her hand firmly but with a slightly nervous smile, as if trying to fit into a situation he wasn't entirely familiar with yet.

The conversation shifted to the foosball table, and within minutes, everyone joined in to play. Amidst laughter and competitive banter, Leo quickly integrated into the group, proving himself not only a good player but also easygoing and likable.

After a few rounds, Leo suddenly stood up and looked around, as if noticing something for the first time. "Anyone want anything from the bar? I'm grabbing something for myself," he offered with a broad smile, now a bit more confident.

Everyone except Brooke responded with a "no, thanks," still absorbed in the game.

Brooke, feeling thirsty, hesitated for a moment. "I'll come with you," she finally said. "I want to see what they have to drink."

Leo nodded with a smile. “Alright, let’s go,” he said, relieved not to head to the bar alone.

They walked to the bar together, the music wrapping around their conversation.

As they waited, they exchanged a glance, and for some reason, a comfortable silence filled the air. Leo broke the ice.

“So, how long have you been in town?” Leo asked, trying to be friendly.

Brooke chuckled nervously. “A while. Honestly, I never thought I’d stay this long in this town. You come here looking for something different, but it seems like I always end up in the same place, you know? Half-finished things, living without really living," she replied, letting out a soft laugh, as if she couldn't help but acknowledge the irony.

Leo studied her for a moment before responding. "Yeah, I get it. I came looking for the same thing—something more. And, well, here I am, doing what I can for now. It's not ideal, but at least it gives me time to think about what I want to do next."

"And what do you think you want to do next?" Brooke asked, genuinely curious but not expecting much from his answer.

Leo shrugged. "I honestly don't know. Maybe travel, see more of the world. Or maybe I'll stay here a bit longer and see what happens." His tone was relaxed, but there was an undercurrent of uncertainty in his words, as if he were still searching for something but didn't know what it was.

Brooke nodded, recognizing that feeling. "Sometimes, I think we stay in the same place out of fear of moving, even though we know we need something different. And sometimes the scariest thing is the change itself," she said, her gaze drifting to the bar, as if searching for answers in the fogged glass.

"Yeah, maybe. Change is scary, but sometimes we don't have another choice," Leo said, not offering many details, but his tone suggested there was more to his words. “Or maybe we just need to learn to embrace that fear.”

“I’m not sure I even want to try,” Brooke replied, letting out a resigned sigh that might have sounded sad but carried a faint trace of hope.

They both fell silent for a moment as Leo paid for the drinks. They returned to the group, which was still playing and laughing. Deep down, Brooke realized that, while she wasn’t exactly happy, talking to Leo had made her feel a little better after everything that had happened lately.

The rest of the night passed quickly, and before they knew it, it was time to leave. Erick offered Brooke and Leo a ride since neither of them had a car that night.

“Need a lift?” Erick asked, grabbing his car keys.

“Yes, please,” Brooke said, relieved she wouldn’t have to walk home. Leo nodded in agreement.

The ride to Brooke’s place was quiet, but a few blocks from her destination, Erick pulled into a darker street and rolled down the window slightly.

“Anyone up for some fun?” Erick asked, glancing at Leo in the rearview mirror and then at Brooke in the passenger seat. “I’ve got weed.”

Brooke and Leo exchanged surprised looks. They knew it was illegal in that country, but both accepted, intrigued by the offer.

"I don't usually do this, but why not? Tonight's not a bad night to try," Leo said, laughing nervously.

Brooke looked at him and smiled, though she wasn't entirely sure what she was thinking. "I guess a little won't hurt. Besides, tonight's the night for trying new things, right, Leo?"

"Yeah. That's the deal we made," Leo said, sounding excited.

"It's just weed. You're making such a fuss over it," Erick teased with a mocking tone.

Erick pulled out a small pouch, lit the joint, and passed it around. Leo was the first to take a puff, then handed it to Brooke. As she inhaled, the cold night air seemed a little lighter. The marijuana relaxed her and cleared her mind for a few moments.

"You know," Leo said, his voice deeper than before, "sometimes I feel like the world is so full of noise, but it's only because no one takes a moment to be quiet. To think about what really matters."

Brooke looked at him, feeling his words resonate within her. "It's true. The noise never really stops. Maybe that's what suffocates us," she said, reflecting for a moment. "Maybe the key is to stop waiting for everything to change and start changing ourselves. Even if that's scary."

"Maybe it's not about changing, but learning to live with what we already have. Learning to find peace in who we already are," Leo replied, staring out the window.

Brooke nodded, her thoughts slightly clearer, though still uncertain. Their conversation led to a comfortable silence, where all three reflected on the lives they were building—or breaking apart—at that very moment.

As smoke floated through the car and the weight of their words lingered in the air, Erick suddenly interrupted with a loud laugh. “Man! I give you a joint, and you turn into Aristotle and Plato.”

Brooke and Leo burst into laughter along with him, letting the seriousness of the moment fade away.

“Alright, time to get back to reality. I need to drop Brooke off at her place; I’ve got work early tomorrow,” Erick said, turning the steering wheel to head back on route.

When they arrived, Brooke opened the car door and said her goodbyes.
"Thanks for the ride, Erick. Take care, you two."

"See you soon, Brooke," Leo said with a sincere smile.

Brooke returned his smile as she stepped out. "See you, Leo. Take care."

As the car drove away, Brooke stood on the sidewalk for a few seconds, feeling how the night had taken an unexpected turn. Something within her had shifted, even if it was just a small step toward something more.

Chapter 2. The Rise

The following week, during her work shift, Erick invited Brooke and Leo to an event that sounded fun. A DJ would be playing music on a mountain, and sleds would be available for sliding down a hill. Everything was free, so the plan couldn't have sounded better. Leo agreed without hesitation.

Brooke, on her part, had begun trying to be more positive about life. Besides, with her closest friends about to move away, making new connections wouldn't hurt. After thinking it over, she accepted the invitation.

At least now she had something to look forward to for the weekend.

The day of the event arrived. When they got there, they noticed there was an open bar—something Erick and Leo took full advantage of, drinking excessively while laughing and hyping each other up. Brooke, on the other hand, played the role of the responsible friend and stuck to sparkling water, though that didn't stop her from enjoying her friends' antics.

As they watched a group trying to cram onto a sled far too small for them, Erick commented:
"You know what that looks like? A live tutorial on how to lose your dignity in three seconds."

Leo burst out laughing.

"And you think you've got dignity left after three tequilas?" Brooke replied, raising an eyebrow.

"Of course! But I left it at the bar with my jacket, just in case I lose it on the hill," Erick retorted, raising his glass dramatically, making everyone laugh.

Later, Leo decided to join the line for sledding down the hill. Brooke tried to warn him.

"Leo, I don't think this is a good idea. You've had a few too many beers."

"Meh! What's the worst that can happen? Besides, I've got great

balance... well, when I'm not so drunk," Leo said with a slurred voice.
"Let him go. It'll be fun," Erick chimed in.

Brooke sighed but didn't try to stop him. She knew Leo wouldn't listen anyway.

As Leo slid down the hill, the group's laughter quickly turned to worry. The sled lost control and crashed into a tree. The impact was hard, and although Leo tried to get up immediately, Brooke noticed something was wrong. When she approached, she saw blood dripping from his wrist, where a sharp branch had made a deep cut.

"Leo, don't move! You're bleeding a lot," Brooke said, feeling panic rise in her throat.
"Is it bad?" Leo asked, a mix of nerves and alcohol clouding his judgment.
"Yes, it is. Erick, we need help right now."

While Erick ran off to find assistance, Brooke knelt beside Leo, pressing her scarf against the wound to try to stop the bleeding. The cold night air made everything feel more surreal, but Brooke stayed calm, though her mind kept repeating how thin the line was between fun and tragedy.

They ended up in the hospital waiting room, with Leo sitting on a gurney as the nurses cleaned his wound and prepared stitches. Erick and Brooke, seated in a corner, exchanged glances that were equal parts worried and resigned.

"I told you it wasn't a good idea," Brooke muttered, crossing her arms.
"Yeah, sure, Mom," Erick replied sarcastically.

When Leo finally came out, his wrist was bandaged, and his mood, against all odds, seemed intact. He walked over to them with a broad smile, as if he had just left a spa instead of the hospital.

"So? Where are we going next?" he said, feigning excitement with his most mocking tone.

Brooke stared at him, incredulous. “What? Not even the accident sobered you up?”

Leo laughed and raised his good hand in an innocent gesture. “Nope, I’m fine now. But look, between what I’ll have to pay for this hospital, the two weeks I won’t be able to work, and being so far from home... if I let myself get sad about this, I’d already be lost.”

Brooke remained silent, trying to process what she had just heard. That response, so full of optimism and pragmatism, was the last thing she expected from someone who had just crashed into a tree at full speed.

"That makes no sense," she finally said, her tone dry. "You should be angry, or worried, or... something."

Leo shrugged. "Why? Do you think being upset will fix anything? I'd rather laugh at my bad luck and move on."

Erick, who had been silent until then, added with a laugh, "That's why the tree hit him. Fate didn't know how to take down someone so positive."

They all laughed, even Brooke, though her laughter was brief and more out of courtesy. Something about Leo's words echoed in her, and not in a comfortable way. She was so used to seeing the gray side of everything that she had never considered facing misfortunes with that kind of attitude as a viable option.

On the way home, Brooke sat silently in the back seat of Erick's car, with Leo dozing off beside her. She stared out the window, watching the snow fall under the streetlights. For the first time in a long while, a question circled her mind: What would happen if I tried to see things the way Leo does? Would anything change, or would I just be lying to myself?

Leo's contagious laughter lingered in her head, mixed with his words. "If I let myself be sad about this, I'd already be lost." Something so simple yet so foreign to her way of thinking.

Chapter 3. Not Everything Has to Go Right

For a few weeks, Brooke had kept her spirits high, doing more than usual. She joined a gym, picked up hobbies, and started planning weekend activities. She'd gone from being cooped up 24/7 to trying to view the world with a more positive attitude. Although she still wasn't clear on what she wanted to do with her life, she was determined to work on herself and improve.

At work, the changes were noticeable, and her coworkers picked up on them.

"Brooke, you're like a different person!" one of her colleagues remarked while they prepared a room. "You used to be the queen of bad moods."

"And now what am I? The princess of good vibes?" Brooke replied sarcastically, though with a genuine smile.

"No, seriously, you seem... I don't know, more alive. What happened?"

"I just decided to stop complaining so much and start doing things. It's either that or keep feeling miserable."

Her coworkers laughed, and Brooke felt a small sense of satisfaction. The changes were still fragile, but they were real.

After work, she headed to her pottery class. Trying new hobbies didn't mean she was overly enthusiastic about them, but Brooke found the sessions therapeutic. She was focused on shaping a small vase when a commotion caught her attention. Turning around, she saw a new guy struggling to keep a piece of clay from spinning out of control on the wheel. His terrified expression as he battled the centrifugal force was so absurd that Brooke had to stifle a laugh.

"Help? I think this thing hates me!" the guy said, raising his clay-covered hands in defeat.

Brooke stood up, amused. "You just have to take control. Let me show you before it explodes."

He stepped back, surrendering the wheel with a grateful smile. "Thanks. I'm Chris, by the way. And you must be the savior of the day."

"Brooke," she replied as she skillfully tamed the spinning clay and shaped it within seconds. "The key is patience. And a bit of practice, of course."

"Patience, got it. But I'm not promising anything," Chris joked, awkwardly wiping his hands on a rag that immediately became unusable.

"If you survive this class without breaking anything, that'll already be progress."

They spent the rest of the time exchanging lighthearted comments and a few laughs, especially when Chris ended up with more clay on his face than on his project. As they left the studio, he caught up with her at the door.

"Thanks for saving me from complete humiliation. Do you come to these classes often?"

"Every Thursday. You?"

"If you promise not to laugh at my attempts, I might start coming every Thursday too."

Brooke gave him a playful look. "No promises."

"Maybe we should hang out this weekend. Got plans?" Chris asked, sounding hopeful.

"Maybe next weekend. I've already got plans with some friends," she replied.

"Sure, we'll plan it later. See you next Thursday!"

That little encounter left her with a good feeling.

On her way home, an unexpected call lit up her phone. The name Rowan, her brother, appeared on the screen. They hadn't spoken in over six months, not out of animosity but because they'd always been a distant family. But something felt off; they usually communicated through brief, practical messages, not phone calls.

"Rowan? Is everything okay?"

"Hi, Brooke. Are you busy?" His tone was heavy, restrained, and it sent a chill down her spine.

"No, why? What's going on?"

There was a pause, as if Rowan were searching for the right words.

“It’s Mom...”

Brooke felt a jolt in her chest before hearing the rest.

“What happened?” Her voice was already trembling.

“She passed away a few hours ago.”

“What? What do you mean she passed away?! She was fine, she was fine...”

“She had a terrible headache this morning and started seeing blurry. I rushed her to the hospital, but she lost consciousness on the way. By the time we got there, they ran tests... but there was nothing they could do. No brain activity. The doctors said it was an aneurysm."

Brooke remained silent, as if her mind couldn't process the words.

"But... Mom was young. She always took care of herself, exercised, ate well. This doesn't make sense, Rowan! It doesn't make any sense!"

"I know, Brooke. I know..." Her brother's voice cracked, and in that moment, Brooke realized she wasn't alone in her grief.

Tears started streaming down her face, silent at first, then uncontrollable. All she could think about was how sudden, absurd, and unfair it was.

“What are we going to do now?”

“First, the funeral. Come home. Little sister, we need you. You need to be here too...”

She nodded, even though Rowan couldn’t see her. She felt something inside her had irreparably shattered.

As she hung up, her mind filled with memories: her mother’s laughter, the small life lessons she would share, how she was always there for Brooke, even in her darkest times. Now, all of that felt so distant.

She wandered aimlessly for a while, unable to return home right away. She couldn’t accept what had just happened, but deep down, she knew life would never be the same.

Chapter 4. Guilt of the Past

It was a scorching summer in her hometown. The dense air and dusty streets seemed to trap the heat in an endless cycle, making time crawl by. Brooke, as always, sought refuge in her room—the only corner where she felt she could breathe without being judged. She had learned to tread carefully around her father, a man whose voice always carried a tone of criticism, as if her mere existence warranted reproach. But she endured it. It was all she had ever known, and in the worst moments, her mother was there to console her, to remind her she wasn't completely alone.

However, that summer, when she was 14, her life changed forever.

It was an afternoon like any other, until it wasn't. Her father's hurtful words met resistance for the first time. Brooke, driven by a rage she didn't know existed within her, stood up to him. What began as just another argument turned into an event that would forever mark not only her relationship with her father but also how she saw the world—and herself.

That afternoon, Brooke was in charge of washing the dishes, as usual. She had put off the task all morning, distracted by a book she'd found at the school library. The sun was at its peak when her father walked into the kitchen and saw the sink still full. His brow furrowed, and Brooke, hearing his heavy footsteps, knew something was about to explode.

“Really? Again? Is it too much to ask for you to do something you’re supposed to do?” His voice boomed through the house, mingling with the hum of the fan. “You’re useless, Brooke. You never do anything right. You’ll never amount to anything.”

Those words, which once made her lower her head and silently endure, this time ignited something inside her. Years of bottled-up anger finally found an outlet.

“And you’re an asshole, and you always will be!” Brooke shouted, her voice trembling with both fury and fear.

The silence that followed was heavier than any blow. Without waiting for his reaction, Brooke stormed out of the house, slamming the door behind her. Her breathing was ragged, her hands trembling. She wanted to get as far away as possible but didn't make it far.

The front door burst open, and her father stormed out after her, his face red with rage.

He caught up to her quickly, and without a word, grabbed her by the hair and yanked her forcefully to the ground. Brooke fell onto her back, the impact filling her body with pain and humiliation.

"Who are you calling an asshole?" he shouted through gritted teeth as she struggled to break free from his grip.

Neighbors began to peek out, but no one dared intervene—until an older man, a construction worker working on a remodel next door, dropped his tools and ran toward them.

"Let her go!" the man yelled, shoving Brooke's father hard enough to make him stumble. But fate, cruel and ironic, had unexpected plans.

Her father tripped over the construction materials piled nearby and fell backward, hitting the back of his head on a loose brick.

The sound was sharp, chilling.

For a moment, everything went silent.

Brooke froze, staring at her father lying motionless on the ground. The man who had defended her tried to revive him, but it was clear something serious had happened.

Minutes later, the sound of ambulance sirens broke the silence, but the damage was already done.

That night, as Brooke waited for news at the hospital, the weight of guilt began to settle on her chest. No matter how much she justified her actions or how many times her mother told her it wasn't her fault, a part of her always blamed herself.

Even though he had crossed the line and physically attacked her, she never wanted her father to die like that.
Brooke deeply understood that her father hadn't treated her that way by choice but because he himself had carried a past filled with hardship and violence. It wasn't hard to imagine a broken child, shaped by rejection and abuse, who had grown up never learning how to give love. But no matter how much she understood the origin of his behavior, it didn't justify it.

She loved him, yes—because he was her father. Because despite everything, a part of her had always hoped to find something more in him than yelling and reproaches—maybe a kind gesture, a word of encouragement. But that love was never enough to fill the void he had left in her life.

Brooke had never had a pillar in him, never a figure who showed her how to feel safe or loved. During her fourteen years under the same roof, her father had been physically present but never emotionally. Living with him was like living with a stranger she dared not approach, for the risk of being hurt was far too great.

That absence disguised as presence had marked Brooke in ways she didn't understand until much later. It wasn't just the lack of a loving father; it was the emptiness of not knowing what it meant to have a paternal figure who believed in her, who was there to catch her when she fell. What hurt the most wasn't the physical harm or the insults but the lost opportunities to have something better —something she now knew she would never be able to reclaim.

With her mother's death, Brooke felt completely broken. Her mother had been her last refuge, the only person who had shown her unconditional love. Now, with her gone, the sense of abandonment was unbearable.

To make matters worse, she hadn't seen her mother in three months or even bothered to call her. That guilt consumed her. If she had known it would be the last time she saw her, she would have done everything differently. But time couldn't be reclaimed.

Chapter 5. The World Doesn't Stop for You

Brooke had returned from her hometown after organizing her mother's funeral and fulfilling her final wish: cremation, just as her mother had always requested. Now, sitting at her desk on a Monday, everything felt empty. It wasn't just the muted colors of the office; life itself felt gray. Hobbies, distractions, and illusions about what her future could hold no longer had a place in her mind. What was the point of moving forward?

The day dragged on slowly, and her coworkers glanced at her with a mix of respect and sadness. They only offered their condolences, unsure how to comfort her. They chose to give her space.

Erick, noticing she hadn't brought her usual coffee, approached Leo with an idea. He suggested they bring her something, knowing that words would never be enough. What Brooke needed—though she wouldn't admit it—was a gesture. So, they went to the café and got her favorite coffee along with a small pastry. They didn't know if it was what she needed, but they thought it might do her some good.

When they returned and handed her the coffee and pastry during lunch, Brooke looked at them, her eyes full of bitterness. With sarcasm in her voice, she said, "If you're going to reward me like this every time a close relative dies, maybe I should hope for more family members to go soon."

Erick and Leo fell silent, clearly uncomfortable with her comment. Without a word, they walked away.

Brooke watched them leave, a faint pang of regret crossing her mind. Maybe she had gone too far, but then again, did having a dead parent give her the right to be an asshole, even just for a little while?

After lunch, Clara, her boss, explained a new procedure for the end of their shifts. Brooke would now need to send a detailed email to her coworkers about everything that had happened during her shift to improve communication and maintain continuity.

But Brooke saw it as the perfect moment to unleash her frustration, albeit in the wrong place at the wrong time.

She began yelling at Clara, telling her she wouldn't do more than she already did unless they considered giving her the raise she had been requesting for a while. "And if you don't like it, do whatever you want."

Clara, trying to remain understanding of Brooke's situation, replied calmly, "Look, I know you're going through a tough time, but these instructions and others we haven't implemented yet are coming from the new company that owns the spa. We're trying to meet certain standards to integrate efficiently into the chain."

"They can shove those standards wherever they want. How's that for meeting expectations?" Brooke snapped, visibly angry.

"I'm going to pretend you didn't say that. Go home. You need to rest," Clara said firmly but seriously.

Brooke, still fuming, left work with no clear destination.

Beatriz had been trying to call Brooke multiple times, but her calls kept going to voicemail. It had been a while since they last talked, but she knew Brooke had returned to the city after her mother's funeral. The lack of response filled her with worry, so she decided to call Brooke's workplace.

Erick answered the phone:
"Riffelalp Resort, how can we help you today?"

"Hi, this is Beatriz, a friend of Brooke. I'm trying to reach her— is she there?"

There was a brief pause before Erick cautiously replied,
"Well... she left early today. There was a bit of an incident."

Erick's tone made Beatriz even more concerned.
"What kind of incident? Is she okay?"

"Let's just say she had a disagreement with Clara, her boss. She hasn't been doing well lately, and they decided it would be best for her to go home and rest."

Beatriz didn't know how to interpret that response. Determined to find her, she asked, "Do you know where she went?"

"No, sorry. I tried calling her later, but she didn't pick up either."

Beatriz hung up, growing more anxious. She couldn't just sit idly by, so she called Joseph, their other childhood friend. "Brooke isn't answering, and she left work early. Something feels off. Can you help me look for her?"

Joseph agreed immediately, and they came up with a plan. First, they checked her house, but it was empty. Then they tried the gym she used to go to, but no one had seen her. They went to other places she frequented but had no luck. Finally, as they drove in silence, Beatriz remembered something.

"The bar. The one we always went to after work... Do you think she could be there?"

Joseph nodded.

"It's worth a shot."

With renewed determination, they headed to the bar, hoping to find her.

When they arrived, Brooke was there, noticeably drunk but with a wide smile, surrounded by strangers as she played pool and laughed like nothing mattered. Beatriz and Joseph exchanged a tense look before approaching her.

"Brooke, finally. We were worried... why weren't you answering?" Beatriz tried to sound calm, though her tone betrayed her anxiety.

Brooke lifted her half-empty glass and, with drunken enthusiasm, replied, "I was busy having fun with my new friends."

Joseph hung back a few steps, crossing his arms and watching cautiously, like someone expecting a storm to break.

"Having fun?" Beatriz replied, trying to keep her composure. "You could at least let us know next time. You left us worried, out of touch. We're your friends, Brooke. We're here for you."

Brooke set the pool cue on the table and turned to face her, her eyes glassy but focused.
"For how long?"

Beatriz froze.
"What do you mean? Always!"

"I don't believe that," Brooke said with unexpected firmness, her words cutting through the air like a knife. "Soon you'll leave. Then, routine will consume you, and you'll talk to me less and less... until we eventually stop talking altogether."

"It doesn't have to be that way!" Beatriz insisted, urgency in her voice. "Joseph, say something, please."

Joseph sighed, lowering his gaze before meeting Brooke's. His tone was firm but without anger, more like exhaustion.
"No, Beatriz, why does it always have to be this way? Why do we have to beg her when we've never been bad friends to her? Brooke, don't you see that most of

the problems in your life come from you? From how you react?"

Brooke felt something inside her shatter. Joseph's words hit where it hurt most, validating the guilt she had been silently carrying—the work issues, the broken relationships, the constant dissatisfaction, her father's death, and the emptiness left by her mother. Neither Beatriz nor Joseph knew how her father had died, but those words felt like a bullet straight to her deepest wound.

With a trembling voice, she tried to keep up her facade:

"I already know I cause my own problems and everyone else's. And you know what? I don't need you. Either of you. I don't need friends who remind me how messed up I am."

Her voice cracked at the end, revealing a pain even the alcohol couldn't mask. Joseph and Beatriz looked at her, unsure whether to approach or step back. Brooke, with tears threatening to fall but refusing to let them, grabbed her jacket and stumbled out of the bar, leaving behind a deafening silence.

Outside, the cold air hit Brooke, waking her partially from her drunken haze. Across the street, she saw Leo walking quickly, hunching against the cold.

"Leooo! Buddy! How are you?" she shouted, her tone a mix of drunken cheer and chaos. Without waiting for a response, she hurried across the street to catch up with him.

Leo greeted her with a warm but slightly uncomfortable smile.
"Good, and you?"

"Awful, and not just because I say so. I have witnesses to prove it. Where are you going?" she asked, leaning toward him slightly, unsteady.

"I'm heading to my other job," Leo replied firmly, not breaking his stride.

Brooke paused, surprised.
"Another one? You're crazy! You haven't even gotten your bandages off, and you're still working."

Leo let out a small laugh. "Well, dreams are expensive... and I don't want to be broke like you forever," he said teasingly, giving her a quick glance.

Brooke let out a genuine laugh and shook her head. "You're an ass. You know I'm having a hard time, and you still talk to me like that. I like you."

"Well, I've got to keep going. I'm already late." Leo checked his watch, quickening his pace toward the bus stop.

As he walked away, Brooke watched his figure fade under the streetlights. Her thoughts swirled, as if the cold had cleared the fog in her mind.

"Maybe I should be more like Leo," she thought as she hugged herself against the chill. He always seemed busy, always building something. But what was he really building? A career? A dream? Or just a way to fill the void, like her?

The echo of his steps disappeared into the night, while Brooke stood there, under the flickering light of a streetlamp, wondering if she would ever find her way out of the hole she felt she had dug for herself.

Joseph's car screeched to a halt in front of her. The window rolled down slowly, revealing his exasperated face.

"Get in, Brooke. Let's take you home before you trip and end up frozen in a ditch somewhere."

Without responding, Brooke opened the back door and slumped into the seat, shutting it with a slam. She crossed her arms and stared out the window, saying nothing the entire ride. The tension was palpable, filling the air with an unbearable weight.
With renewed determination, they headed to the bar, hoping to find her.

When they arrived, Brooke was there, noticeably drunk but with a wide smile, surrounded by strangers as she played pool and laughed like nothing mattered. Beatriz and Joseph exchanged a tense look before approaching her.

"Brooke, finally. We were worried… why weren't you answering?" Beatriz tried to sound calm, though her tone betrayed her anxiety.

Brooke lifted her half-empty glass and, with drunken enthusiasm, replied, "I was busy having fun with my new friends."

Joseph hung back a few steps, crossing his arms and watching cautiously, like someone expecting a storm to break.

"Having fun?" Beatriz replied, trying to keep her composure. "You could at least let us know next time. You left us worried, out of touch. We're your friends, Brooke. We're here for you."

Brooke set the pool cue on the table and turned to face her, her eyes glassy but focused.

"For how long?"

Beatriz froze.

"What do you mean? Always!"

"I don't believe that," Brooke said with unexpected firmness, her words cutting through the air like a knife. "Soon you'll leave. Then, routine will consume you, and you'll talk to me less and less... until we eventually stop talking altogether."

"It doesn't have to be that way!" Beatriz insisted, urgency in her voice. "Joseph, say something, please."

Joseph sighed, lowering his gaze before meeting Brooke's. His tone was firm but without anger, more like exhaustion.
"No, Beatriz, why does it always have to be this way? Why do we have to beg her when we've never been bad friends to her? Brooke, don't you see that most of the problems in your life come from you? From how you react?"

Brooke felt something inside her shatter. Joseph's words hit where it hurt most, validating the guilt she had been silently carrying—the work issues, the broken relationships, the constant dissatisfaction, her father's death, and the emptiness left by her mother. Neither Beatriz nor Joseph knew how her father had died, but those words felt like a bullet straight to her deepest wound.

With a trembling voice, she tried to keep up her facade:
"I already know I cause my own problems and everyone else's. And you know what? I don't need you. Either of you. I don't need friends who remind me how messed up I am."

Her voice cracked at the end, revealing a pain even the alcohol couldn't mask. Joseph and Beatriz looked at her, unsure whether to approach or step back. Brooke, with tears threatening to fall but refusing to let them, grabbed her jacket and stumbled out of the bar, leaving behind a deafening silence.

As she left the bar, the cold air hit Brooke, partially waking her from the lethargy of alcohol. Across the street, she saw Leo walking quickly, hunched over to shield himself from the cold.

"Leooo! Buddy! How are you?" she shouted, her tone a mix of drunken joy and recklessness. Without waiting for an answer, she hurried across the street to catch up with him.

Leo greeted her with a warm but slightly awkward smile.
"I'm good. And you?"

"Terrible, and not just because I say so. There are witnesses to prove it. Where are you going?" she asked, leaning slightly toward him, unsteady.

“I’m heading to my other job,” Leo replied firmly but kept walking.

Brooke stopped for a moment, surprised.
“Another one? You’re crazy! They haven’t even taken off the bandage, and you’re already working again.”

Leo let out a small laugh. “Well, dreams are expensive… and I don’t want to be poor like you my whole life,” he said teasingly, throwing her a quick glance.

Brooke let out a genuine laugh and shook her head.
“You bastard. You know I’m struggling, and you still talk to me like that. I like you.”

"Well, I've got to go. I'm already late," Leo said, glancing at his watch and quickening his pace toward the bus stop.

As he walked away, Brooke watched his figure blur under the yellow streetlights. Her thoughts began to swirl, as if the cold had cleared some of the fog in her mind.

"Maybe I should be more like Leo," she thought as she hugged her arms to keep warm. He always seemed busy, always building something. But what was he really building? A career? A dream? Or just a way to fill the void, just like her?

The echo of his footsteps faded into the night, leaving Brooke standing under the flickering light of a streetlamp, wondering if she would ever climb out of the hole she felt she had dug for herself.

Joseph's car screeched to a halt in front of her. The window rolled down slowly, revealing his exasperated face.

"Get in, Brooke. Let's get you home before you trip and freeze in some ditch."

Without replying, Brooke opened the back door and slumped into the seat, slamming it shut. The entire ride, she sat with her arms crossed, staring out the window, silent. The tension was palpable, the air heavy with discomfort.

When they arrived, Brooke got out without even glancing back at them. She barely muttered a dry "Thanks," devoid of any sincerity.

Joseph, gripping the steering wheel tightly, watched as she closed the door to her house without saying goodbye. Then, turning to Beatriz, he let out a tired sigh.

"Leave her be, Beatriz. She wants to stay down, and if she insists on that, there's nothing we can do. But don't let her drag you down too."

Beatriz stared at Brooke's closed door, her eyes glistening with sadness and a hint of helplessness. But she said nothing. Joseph's words weighed on her because, painful as they were, they rang true.

Chapter 6: The Abyss

Brooke was beginning to feel like a shadow of herself. There was something dark looming over her, as if it was devouring her from within. It wasn't a physical illness, but the emotional toll was destroying her. Day by day, she sank further into a routine—a routine that felt empty and painful. She stopped going out with friends, gave up activities she once enjoyed, and refused invitations from those who tried to reach out. She was trapped in a cycle of self-imposed isolation, growing increasingly disconnected from others and from herself.

During lunch at work, Leo sat alone with his headphones on, staring blankly as he ate his fast food. He looked relaxed, but it wasn't hard to see that, like everyone else, he felt the weight of routine. Unable to bear the silence, Brooke walked over and sat beside him.

"I'm so tired of this place," Brooke said, her voice heavy with exhaustion. "Don't you get tired of this job and this place?"

Leo glanced at her briefly but kept eating.
"Yeah, of course. There's not much to do here. At least going out and doing something keeps me distracted."

Brooke crossed her arms and watched as Leo seemed so calm while she felt increasingly trapped.
"But when do you ever go out if you're working all the time?"

"Well, honestly, I don't go out much either, but enough... I think," Leo replied calmly. "If I don't give myself some free time, I start to get frustrated. I try a bit of everything—parties, trips to nearby towns... even though I don't do it as often as I should, there are so many things on my bucket list that I still haven't done. Actually, I'm going on a hike near town this weekend. Wanna come?"

Brooke looked at him, the idea of going out feeling foreign, something she wasn't sure she could still do.
"I've lived here for a while, and I think I've only been to a couple of places. Maybe it wouldn't be so bad."

There was something in her words that hinted at a spark of hope, but also a deep disconnection. Leo's invitation was a reminder that there was something beyond her bubble of pain and emptiness. Why not try? Something inside her, though faint, responded to the idea. Maybe, just maybe, going on a hike, breathing in some fresh air, could make things feel different, even if just for a moment. But that spark of interest quickly faded, replaced by the weight of doubt. What's the point of trying? The apathy constantly fought to take over.

The contrast between her and Leo couldn't have been starker. He still clung to small escapes, moments of distraction that kept him afloat. Meanwhile, Brooke felt dragged down, unable to find anything that pushed her forward. In her mind, the hike was nothing more than an illusion, something she might want to do but couldn't find the motivation for.

Despite a small part of her wanting to go, the rest had already decided that nothing was worth it. After all, there were so many reasons to give up, so many wounds that wouldn't heal.

Maybe, she thought, it was easier to keep sinking.

The morning of the hike came. Brooke, still in her pajamas and pale from the winter cold, felt her phone vibrate on the nightstand. It was Leo.

“Hey, the bus to the trail leaves in an hour. Are you coming?” Leo’s tone was cheerful, in stark contrast to Brooke’s grogginess.

Brooke sighed deeply, staring at the ceiling. Another day in this endless cycle, she thought.
“Fine. You woke me up already. I’ll see you at the bus,” she replied, her voice tinged with indifference.

Still half-asleep, she put on the warmest clothes she could find and left her apartment, her mind clouded by exhaustion. The mountain winter was unforgiving, and the cold breeze that hit her face as she stepped outside reminded her how bleak everything felt.

When they reached the trail, they started walking in silence, the freezing air biting at their skin. Leo walked with energy, despite the cold, taking photos and admiring the snowy landscape.

"What do you think about death?" Brooke asked, her voice broken by the wind as she watched her bootprints mark the snow.

Leo glanced at her, surprised, but kept walking. “Well, the farther away, the better. Death scares me. I don’t know... maybe I’m just not ready to face it.”

Brooke smirked grimly, her eyes fixed on the falling snow. “To me, death seems like the only thing that could free me from this. In the end, we were dust, and we’ll return to dust. It’s a cycle. Don’t you see? Like a well-deserved rest.”

Leo stopped for a moment, frowning. “Seriously? Have you never thought that maybe life has more to offer than giving up like that?”

Brooke shrugged, walking slowly to catch up with him. “Life doesn’t have much to offer me. Everything feels empty. Maybe death is the last act of control I can have. And at least it would be peaceful."

Leo looked at her with concern. "I don't understand, Brooke. I want to make the most of every second I have left. I don't want to go so soon. Death... it terrifies me."

"I see it differently," she replied, pulling a pill out of her backpack and swallowing it quickly with a sip of water. Leo watched her, his face creased with curiosity.

"What's that? Are you sick?" he asked, raising an eyebrow.

Brooke gave him a quick glance, brushing off the question. “It’s just vitamins,” she replied indifferently, not putting much effort into the lie.

At the end of the trail, when they reached a viewpoint, the snowy landscape seemed endless. The stillness of winter contrasted with the turbulence in Brooke’s mind. Leo, however, smiled with admiration for the view, taking more photos.

“What do you think happens after death?” Brooke asked as they both stopped at the edge of the snowy cliff.

Leo hesitated for a moment, looking at the horizon, as if searching for an answer in the cold emptiness of the snow. “I don’t know. Maybe something, maybe nothing. I don’t like to think that after everything we live, it just ends. The idea of nothing terrifies me, that all the effort and emotions just disappear.”

Brooke stayed silent for a moment. “That scares you, huh? It doesn’t bother me. If it ends, it ends. I’m not afraid.”

Leo turned to look at her but said nothing else. The atmosphere between them grew heavy. Neither could find a complete answer to the questions tormenting them. For Leo, life was a struggle worth continuing, while for Brooke, death seemed like the only way out of a world that no longer made sense.

As they headed back to the bus, Leo tried to break the silence. “Do you think that when we die, we just stop existing?”

Brooke paused for a moment, looking at the snow covering the path. “I don’t know. And honestly, I don’t care. Maybe we’ll never have answers. But in the meantime, at least I’m not afraid to face it.”

Leo watched her with sadness. “Do you really feel that way?”

“Yes,” she said, almost with an unsettling calmness, “and I prefer it to going in circles in this damned cycle.”

Chapter 7. Brooke Is Broken

December 28 was just another day in the city: snow-covered streets, a cold that cut to the bone, and a hurried pace for the end-of-year festivities. Leo arrived at work a few minutes before his shift, as always. Just as he was entering, he saw Erick helping Brooke out of the building.

Brooke was staggering, her eyes red and sunken, her face pale, and her hair disheveled. She looked like she had drunk heavily the night before. Even her clothes were wrinkled, as if she had grabbed the first thing she found upon waking. Leo couldn't help but frown at the sight of her.

"I'll be back quickly, I'm just taking Brooke home," said Erick without stopping, searching for his keys in his pocket.

Leo watched, confused. "What happened to her? Is she on something?"

"I don't know, but she's in bad shape. I'll drop her off before the boss sees her and fires her for this. Please cover for me," Erick replied, almost pleading, before helping Brooke into the car.

Leo stood there for a few seconds, watching them drive away. Poor Brooke, he thought. She's destroying herself. It's been a couple of months since that strange talk about death, but her attitude has only gotten worse. She's a good friend, but how do you help someone who doesn't want to be helped?

About 30 minutes later, Erick returned, his face filled with worry.

"Well?" asked Leo.

"I left her in bed. She seemed... out of it, asleep or... I don't know. I just hope she rests."

Leo nodded. "You did the right thing. We can't let her get fired over this. Between the two of us, we'll cover for her."

The day went on, but Brooke lingered in his thoughts. Around midday, Leo decided to step out to get lunch. As he crossed the street to a nearby shop, a young man stopped him.

"Excuse me, do you work here?" he asked, holding a small wooden box in his hands.

"Yes, can I help you?" Leo replied.

The young man smiled nervously. "Well... this is a bit weird, but I wanted to ask you a favor. This box is for a girl who works here—Brooke. I'm too shy to give it to her myself... she might take it the wrong way. I thought if someone from her job gave it to her, it would be less awkward."

Leo raised an eyebrow. “For Brooke? Hmm...”

The young man stepped back, worried. “Is it a bad idea? Did I say something wrong?”

Leo noticed his discomfort and quickly clarified, “No, no! I was just saying that because... well, Brooke isn’t here today. Do you want me to give it to her tomorrow?”

The young man sighed in relief. “That’d be great. Look, I’m leaving town for a month to spend New Year’s with my family. If she likes it, tell her it’s from Chris. If not... just say it’s from a secret admirer. That way, if she’s not interested, I won't look like an idiot. Anyway, I won't be here, and when I come back, maybe I'll have another chance to talk to her."

Leo smiled, amused. "Sounds like you've thought this through. I'll make sure she gets it."

Chris seemed more at ease. "Thanks, really. It's just a small gesture, nothing big, but I wanted her to know someone's thinking of her."

"That's nice. I hope she likes it," Leo said, now more curious about the young man. "Do you know her well?"

"We met a couple of months ago. She's... different, you know? There's something special about her. Sad, but special. I just want her to know that someone sees her."

Leo nodded, admiring his honesty. "I promise, I'll make sure she gets the gift."

They said their goodbyes, and Leo returned to work with a small smile. Maybe this guy was what Brooke needed. Hopefully, she could face her storms, though she would need all the strength in the world.

When he returned, Leo placed the box in his locker, forgetting about lunch altogether. His mind was preoccupied with Brooke, Chris, and the sense that something good might happen for her.

After work, Leo grabbed the wooden box from his locker and took the bus to his second job as usual. As the vehicle moved, he gazed distractedly out the window at the beautiful scenery. He thought about calling Brooke to check on her after her rough morning and to let her know he had something for her. However, he decided to put it off. I'll do it after work, when my mind is clearer.

The shift at his second job was more demanding than expected. He barely had time to stop and breathe, and before he knew it, it was 11 p.m. Exhausted, he left the building, and as he waited for the bus, he checked his phone for the first time all afternoon. He noticed a missed call notification.

"Brooke..." he murmured, staring at the screen. He hesitated for a moment but let his exhaustion win. "Not tonight, Brooke, sorry," he whispered, putting his phone back in his pocket. She probably wants to go out drinking or something. I'll talk to her tomorrow.

The ride home felt slow—or at least it did to Leo, his body and mind too fatigued to process time. When he arrived, he left the wooden box on the table and collapsed onto his bed. Sleep overtook him almost instantly, leaving no room even to think about dinner.

The next morning came sooner than Leo would have liked. He woke up with a start, realizing he only had twenty minutes to get to work. He dressed hurriedly, brushed his teeth, and rushed out, barely remembering to grab the small box he still hadn't delivered.

He arrived ten minutes late. To his relief, no one seemed to have noticed his absence, so he slipped into the usual flow of the day. An hour later, Clara broke the silence with a complaint that left the atmosphere tense.

"I can't believe Brooke is skipping work again," she said, slamming a clipboard on the table. "Right in the busiest days. It's unbelievable. This girl thinks she can take vacations whenever she feels like it."

Erick, standing nearby, looked uneasy. He pulled his phone from his pocket and began dialing. "Let me try to reach her," he said, frowning.

He pressed the call button, but the line didn't even ring before going straight to voicemail.

At lunchtime, while everyone else talked about backlogged orders and the day's routine, Erick approached Leo with a serious expression.

"Hey, we should go to Brooke's place. I'm worried. She never skips work, even yesterday when she was drunk, she still came in," he said quietly, trying not to draw attention.

Leo looked up from his plate with an indifferent expression. "Give her some space. She was probably just fed up and didn't want to come in."

"I don't know..." Erick crossed his arms, visibly uneasy. "I have a bad feeling I can't shake."

Leo sighed. "It's nothing. I saw her last night while heading to my other job. She looked bad, but not as bad as in the morning. Plus, she called me in the evening. She was probably going to invite us to drink or something."

"And you didn't answer?" Erick raised an eyebrow.

"I was tired," Leo admitted with a shrug. "This isn't the first time she's done something like this. She'll show up tomorrow."

"No, seriously, Leo," Erick insisted, his tone more firm. "I feel like something's wrong. Let's go to her place."

Leo stared at him for a moment, weighing whether it was worth continuing the discussion. Finally, with a resigned gesture, he set his fork down on the table. "Fine, but when we get there and you realize you're overreacting, you're buying dessert."

"Deal," said Erick without a hint of humor as he pulled his car keys from his pocket.

Before they left, Clara eyed them from across the room. "What's going on now?"

"We're going to check on Brooke," Erick replied without stopping.

Clara scoffed. "You two have more faith in that girl than I have in this place."

Leo smirked sarcastically as they walked out the door. "That's our Clara: ever the optimist."

Erick started the car, and Leo settled into the passenger seat. Though he tried not to show it, his friend's concern was starting to affect him, and an uncomfortable silence filled the space between them as the car moved along the icy streets.

When they reached Brooke's building, Erick knocked on her apartment door several times, each time louder. There was no response or any sign of movement inside. He glanced around nervously and pulled out his phone. After trying to call Joseph and Beatriz, two of Brooke's friends Erick knew, his worry only deepened as neither of them had heard from her.

"This isn't right," he said, looking at Leo.

Erick turned his attention to the side of the building, where Brooke's balcony was just a few meters up.

“I have an idea. Come with me.”

Leo followed him, looking confused. Erick pointed at the balcony. “Climb up there. She never locks the sliding door to the balcony.”

“Climb?” Leo frowned. “Are you serious? You want me to break into her place?”

“It’s not breaking in if we’re worried about her wellbeing. Look, you’re lighter than me. If I try, I’ll probably break something or fall. It’s easier for me to boost you up.”

“I don’t know, Erick... this feels like a really bad idea.”

"Please, Leo. What if something bad happened and we did nothing? I couldn't live with that."

Leo sighed, resigned. "Fine. But you better not tell anyone I did this."

Erick smiled slightly, relieved, and laced his hands together to give Leo a boost. With a jump, Leo managed to grab the edge of the balcony and, with some effort, hoisted himself up. He peeked inside. Just as Erick had said, the door was unlocked.

"I'm going in," Leo murmured before sliding the door open and disappearing into the apartment.

Inside, he walked cautiously, calling out softly, "Brooke? Are you here?" There was no response. After a moment, he made his way to the front door and unlocked it to let Erick in.

"Anything?" Erick asked as he stepped inside.

Leo shook his head. "Nothing. Everything's in its place, but there's no sign she's been here."

They searched every corner of the apartment. The bed was made, the dishes in the sink were clean, and there were no clothes lying around, as if the place had been empty for days.

Erick ran a hand through his hair, frustrated. "This doesn't make sense."

"Maybe she stayed at someone else's place," Leo suggested, though his tone lacked conviction.

As they left the apartment, they got back into the car, exhausted and more worried than before. Erick started the engine, but before driving off, his phone vibrated. It was a message on social media.

"It's from Rowan, Brooke's brother," Erick said, glancing at the screen.

The message read: "Hey, man. Do you know anything about my sister? She sent a strange message yesterday, and I haven't been able to reach her."

Leo, hearing this, leaned toward the driver's seat. "A strange message? What did it say?"

"I don't know, but this confirms something is wrong." Erick clenched his teeth. "We have to go to the police."

After replying to Rowan to explain the situation, they started the car and drove to the police station. Neither of them spoke on the way; the silence was heavy, filled with fear and unanswered questions.

The report was filed that same day, triggering a search involving the police, volunteers, friends, and acquaintances of Brooke. Beatriz, Joseph, Erick, and Leo joined the groups, tirelessly combing through streets, parks, and the city's outskirts. Each day that passed without finding her added a layer of pessimism reflected in their increasingly scarce words and weary looks. Rowan, who arrived on December 30, joined the effort with determination, though sadness and frustration were etched on his face.

That day, while they organized search routes, Rowan gathered Leo, Erick, Beatriz, and Joseph. His tone was serious, almost accusatory.

"Did any of you notice anything strange about Brooke recently?" he asked, crossing his arms and staring at them intently.

Beatriz, nervous, was the first to respond. “Well, yes... lately, she looked exhausted. Like she hadn’t slept in days.”

Joseph added in a low voice, “Sometimes she told me everything felt like too much, but... I thought she just needed time.”

Erick, staring at the ground, confessed, “I noticed she was more distant, but I thought it was better to give her space... I didn’t want to make her uncomfortable.”

Leo sighed before speaking. “I saw her the day before she disappeared. She was walking near work, and she didn’t look that bad. That night she called me, but I didn’t answer because I thought she was going to invite me out, and I was tired...”

Rowan interrupted, his voice shaking with anger. “And no one thought to tell me? No one thought I might need to know? You didn’t even have to help her if you didn’t want to, you just had to tell me! I’m her brother, for God’s sake! If I had known, I would’ve done whatever it took to be here sooner.”

Silence fell among them, heavy as a gravestone. Rowan shook his head in disbelief, clearly fighting back tears. “And now here we are, searching every corner of this city, when all of this could have been avoided."

That afternoon, security camera footage confirmed one of Brooke's last known locations. She was seen walking near the river. Although the clue gave them a clearer target, it also ignited everyone's worst fears. Rowan led the search in the area, scouring every inch with a mix of hope and despair.

On January 2, while the group combed through the area around the river, one of the volunteers found her body. The news spread quickly among the searchers. Rowan was the first to arrive. He stood frozen at the sight of her, as if time had stopped. Then he ran to her, falling to his knees at the riverbank.

"No... Brooke... no..." he murmured before breaking into heart-wrenching sobs. He held her in his arms, ignoring the icy cold of the water, unable to let her go.

Beatriz and Joseph arrived shortly after, but upon seeing the scene, they stopped in their tracks. Rowan lifted his gaze toward them, his eyes filled with pain and fury. "All of this... could have been avoided."

A few minutes later, Erick and Leo came running. Rowan didn't look at them at first, until finally, with a cold voice, he said, "You're late... all of you, you're too late."

His words hung in the air like a condemnation. Erick lowered his head, while Leo tried to speak, but the words simply wouldn't come.

When the authorities arrived to take the body, Rowan stayed with Brooke until the very last moment. The journey back was somber, marked by a silence none of them knew how to break. For Rowan, the loss was twofold: his sister and the certainty that, with a little more attention, everything could have been different.

Chapter 8. Black Snow

Brooke had maintained her usual appearance of sadness and apathy, the kind that made her almost invisible to those around her. But on December 28, something broke. That morning, she arrived at work visibly affected: pale skin, sunken eyes, and slight unsteadiness in her movements betrayed her. She had drunk heavily the night before. Her friend Erick, noticing her condition before the boss could see her like that, decided to help her. He took her home and covered for her, saying she was sick and couldn't come to work.

She spent the entire morning locked in her room, sleeping. However, as the afternoon fell, something drove her to do what she shouldn't have done. According to witnesses, she left her home and spent hours at a local bar, drinking alone. By nightfall, something entirely unexpected and irreversible was about to happen.

Police and Forensic Report on Brooke's Case – January 2, 2021

Date of disappearance: December 29, 2020
Date of discovery: January 2, 2021
Location: Riverbed, mountainous area near the city

General context: Brooke was reported missing on December 29, 2020. Four days later, her body was found in a river about 22 kilometers from where she is believed to have fallen. A combination of factors, including her physical and emotional state and the conditions of the environment, led to a tragic outcome.

Incident details: The night of December 28 was extremely cold, with below-freezing temperatures and ice covering much of the terrain. According to the toxicology report, Brooke had significant levels of alcohol and benzodiazepines in her system. This combination severely impaired her coordination, judgment, and reaction time, leaving her vulnerable in a hostile environment.

Effects of intoxication: The combined use of benzodiazepines and alcohol causes deep sedation, loss of coordination, and a confused mental state. It is likely Brooke was experiencing a mix of physical lethargy, confusion, and diminished danger perception in her final moments.

Last records of activity:

- **10:28 p.m.:** Sent a text to her brother Rowan saying, "I love you, brother."
- **10:32 p.m.:** Called Leo, who did not answer because he was working.

- **10:34 p.m.:** Called Beatriz, but she couldn't answer as she was on a flight.
- **10:47 p.m.:** Made a final call to her mother's number, who had passed away months earlier. Although there was no response, she left a voicemail retrieved during the investigation:

"Mommy, where are you? ... I feel like I'm drowning, Mom. You're going to help me, right? You always help me..."

The audio continued for nine more seconds, capturing the sound of footsteps on snow before ending abruptly.

Body discovery: On January 2, 2021, Brooke's body was found on the riverbank. It showed multiple contusions consistent with impacts against the rocks in the riverbed during the 22 kilometers she was carried by the current.

A peculiar detail noted by rescuers was the presence of a dark pool in the snow around Brooke's head. This phenomenon, which made the snow appear black like an aura around her head, was explained as a mixture of bodily fluids, organic particles from the river, and chemical residues from the substances in her body.

Additional investigation: Therapist under suspicion

During the investigation, a new angle led detectives to look into the sources of the benzodiazepines found in Brooke's system. A recurring connection in the young woman's life was an unlicensed therapist operating on the outskirts of the city. This individual, identified as Martin Calderón, had been offering "therapy sessions" and prescribing controlled substances under the guise of being a psychiatrist.

Calderón, who previously worked as an assistant at a clinic, used falsified credentials and issued prescriptions through contacts at pharmacies that did not verify them. Among his clients were several young people with a history of mental health issues. According to testimonies, Calderón often downplayed the risks of the medications, referring to them as "a little help for tough days."

Although Brooke never openly mentioned Calderón, bank records show recurring payments to his account in the months leading up to her death. This has raised suspicions about whether he indirectly contributed to the deterioration of her mental state through irresponsible prescribing of benzodiazepines.

Forensic conclusion: While it cannot be determined with certainty whether Brooke accidentally fell into the river or made a deliberate decision, the evidence—her intoxication, the message to her brother, the unanswered calls, and her final voicemail—indicates she was in a state of deep emotional confusion.

Brooke's case reflects the dangers of substance abuse and the influence of negligent professionals. Beyond being a personal tragedy, it highlights the need for stricter controls on prescription medications and appropriate support for those facing mental health challenges. It is undeniably tragic that such a young woman lost her life this way.

Chapter 9. Unanswered Letters

March 12, 2021

Dear Future Leo,

It's been three months since Brooke died, and I can't help but wonder how you're doing as you read these words. Better? Worse? Or just the same as now, surviving on autopilot?

Since everything happened, time seems to have turned into an endless shadow. My days are a blur: wake up, work, sleep, and repeat. The routine consumes me, and in a way, that's what I want. I don't think when I'm busy. Silence only comes when I close my eyes at night, and by then, I'm so exhausted I can't stay awake to face the questions waiting for me.

I've started working more than I ever thought possible. If I used to live at work, now I practically breathe there. My shifts stretch on because I stretch them. I take others' overtime, even the hours no one else wants. Anything to fill the voids. Remember how much you hated those long days? Now I chase them desperately.

It's not just work. I've started drinking more than I should. Nothing serious—or at least that's what I tell myself. Just a couple of drinks after a shift. Then a couple more at home. I don't know when it became a habit, but there are nights when I need the warmth of alcohol to keep the memories from creeping in.

It's strange because I always thought time healed everything. But with each passing day, the weight in my chest doesn't go away; it just settles deeper, heavier.

Future Leo, if you're reading this, I hope you've somehow found a purpose to keep going. Because right now, I have no idea how to do it.

With uncertainty,
Present Leo

March 14, 2021

Dear Future Leo,

It's hard to write this because, no matter how much I try, Rowan's voice keeps echoing in my head, refusing to fade. His words, heavy with rage and raw pain, feel like scars that won't heal: *"You didn't even have to help her if you didn't care... you just had to tell me."* I hear them over and over, as if repeating them might change their shape or dull the edge with which they cut. But they don't.

What unsettles me most isn't what Rowan said, though, but what I feel—or rather, what I don't feel. There's no overwhelming flood of guilt, no deep regret. There's just... emptiness.

At first, I tried to convince myself it wasn't my responsibility. Brooke wasn't my family; she wasn't my closest friend; lately, she wasn't even someone I shared much more with than polite greetings and a few trivial moments. She wasn't my problem, or Erick's, or anyone else's but her own. That was the truth I repeated to myself, like a mantra, during the first weeks after her death. But over time, that "truth" started to crumble.

Now I understand guilt doesn't always feel like a direct punch to the chest. There's another kind of guilt, more subtle, more treacherous. It doesn't come from what you did but from what you didn't do. I didn't push her into the abyss, but I also didn't reach out to pull her back. And that absence of action, that silence I let fill the spaces between us, is what weighs on me the most.

I can still see her clearly. Brooke had this way of laughing that seemed genuine, but if you stopped to look into her eyes, you could tell something didn't quite fit. It was like there was an invisible barrier between her and the rest of the world. You know what's most unsettling? I noticed it. I always noticed it. But I never did anything about it.

Erick, on the other hand, has been dealing with this in a completely different way. When Rowan confronted us, it was the first time I saw Erick truly break. I remember his trembling hands, his red eyes, like he was on the verge of collapse. He couldn't hold Rowan's gaze, let alone respond to him. I, on the other hand, just stood there, almost like a spectator of a tragedy that wasn't mine. But that was a lie, wasn't it? It was as much mine as it was Erick's, as much mine as it was Rowan's.

Do you remember how that confrontation ended? Rowan ended up yelling at us, accusing us of being complicit in her death. *"She was my last living family, and you didn't even have the decency to tell me she was in danger!"* Those words have haunted me ever since. Not because I feel guilty, but because I don't know how to process all of this. I don't know what I'm supposed to feel.

Future Leo, did you ever manage to understand any of this? Did you find a way to make peace with yourself? Because I'm still trapped in this state of emptiness, unable to move forward, unable to look back without feeling like there's something terribly wrong with me.

With confusion,
Leo

March 19, 2021

Dear Future Leo,

It's strange how the body starts to rebel when the mind gives up. I've been sleeping less, not because I don't want to, but because it feels like my body and mind are in constant disagreement. When I finally manage to close my eyes, something always forces them open again. Sometimes it's an echo of words I'm not sure are real; other times, it's the sound of my own breathing, which becomes unbearable in the dark.

But even when I do sleep, I wake up disoriented. The dizziness is becoming more frequent, like the world decides to tilt beneath my feet without warning.

The other day, I was in the kitchen trying to drink some water and had to grip the edge of the sink because I felt like I was about to fall. It was brief, but enough to make me realize something is wrong.

Lately, I've noticed something unsettling: my reflection. I pass by the mirrors in the house, and for some reason, I avoid looking at myself. When I do, it feels like I'm staring at a stranger. The eyes staring back at me are dull, empty, and that terrifies me. Is it possible to lose yourself without even realizing it?

A few nights ago, after another bout of insomnia, I stopped in front of the bathroom mirror. I stared at myself, trying to find some trace of the person I used to be before all this. But all I saw was someone suspended between the past and the present, incapable of moving forward.

Sometimes I think about water, about how Brooke let herself be carried away by it. I wonder if I'm also being dragged by something—if this inertia I feel is my way of giving up. But then I get angry at myself because I know I have no right to feel this way. Not after what happened.

Leo, if you ever read this, I hope you recognize yourself in the mirror. I hope you find something I haven't been able to find yet. Because, at least for now, it feels like I'm searching in the wrong place—or maybe searching for something that was never there.

With uncertainty,

Leo

March 21, 2021

Dear Future Leo,

I've been thinking about how the connections I once thought were so strong have slowly unraveled. I remember when I used to talk to my family almost every day. The calls filled with laughter, the messages of support, even the trivial conversations that seemed meaningless. Now, I can hardly remember the last time I replied to one of their messages.

At first, the excuses seemed valid: work, exhaustion, "I'll call them tomorrow." But now I realize I'm isolating myself. I don't even know why. Sometimes I think it's because I'm afraid they'll notice how broken I am. That if I talk to them, I won't be able to hide this version of myself that I no longer recognize. Or maybe it's because I feel so disconnected from everything that words feel useless.

The same thing has happened with friends. The ones who used to reach out have stopped. I don't blame them. What could they possibly find here that's worth their time? I barely respond. And when I do, my replies are cold, automatic, as if a stranger were typing them for me.

I've even lost touch with people from my home country, those I used to share snippets of my life with. The stories, the photos, the jokes... all of that has evaporated. Now there's a void where those connections used to be.

It's ironic. I always thought I was strong, that I could handle anything. But now, the more I withdraw, the weaker I feel. I wonder if you, the Leo reading this someday, will be able to rebuild those bonds. Or if it'll already be too late.

With uncertainty and a glimmer of hope,
Leo

March 27, 2021

Dear Future Leo,

If you're reading this, it means there's still a part of you that believes in change. And that, even if it's small, is enough to build something new.

If I could ask you for one thing, it would be to leave behind this routine that's killing us. I want you to pack a backpack —just one—and go. Forget about luxuries, comforts, or fear of the unknown. I want you to walk paths you've never stepped on, sleep under skies you've never seen, and talk to people whose language you don't even understand at first. I want you to take risks, to feel your heart race for something other than exhaustion or stress.

I want you to remember what it's like to be strong. Not physical strength—not the kind measured in muscles or endurance—but the kind that comes from knowing you can face the world and not give in. I want you to confront the fear of failure, rejection, or not being enough. I want you to try new things, even if they fail, even if they hurt. Because if I've learned anything in these months, it's that the pain of doing nothing is far worse than the pain of trying and failing.

Imagine this: a life full of experiences, not things. Endless walks, laughter with strangers, moments when the wind messes up your hair, and you feel, even for a second, that everything makes sense. I want you to get your hands dirty, feel the sweat run down your face as you climb a mountain, get lost, and find something unexpected.

Do it for me—for this Leo who couldn't, who was trapped in a dark place and didn't know how to get out. Do it for us, for the life we can still have.

I'm not asking you to change everything all at once, but start with one step. One decision. Something to break this cycle. Please don't forget that even though it feels like everything is lost now, there's always a way out. There's always a way to feel alive again.

But who am I kidding? I'll never do any of this. It's just another lie, one that gives me just enough light to keep waiting for something in me to change.

Sincerely,
Leo

March 30, 2021

Dear Future Leo,

It's funny how the city keeps filling up with new people every year. New faces, new stories neither you nor I know, but ones that will probably be just as fleeting. I watch them, their eyes glowing with excitement, so unaware of everything I've carried for so long. They have this energy I barely recognize anymore, as if every corner of this place holds a new opportunity for them. Envy. Envy for how they can see the world with that spark of novelty, as if every street, every corner, is a promise waiting to be discovered.

I wish I had that energy, that ability to start over. But the truth is, I don't feel like this place has anything left to offer me. Every day here is just a repeat of the last. The city doesn't hold anything for me anymore, only memories that follow me, haunt me. And yet, here I stay, because the pay is good, because maybe, deep down, I've stayed because I don't know how to start somewhere else. Money is the only thing that seems to keep me going, but it doesn't make me feel alive anymore. It doesn't even give me what I need to heal.

Sometimes, when I look at these newcomers, I feel like I've lost the right to that kind of excitement. They have their whole lives ahead of them, unmarked by the scars I carry, untouched by the weight that's held me back. I wonder if sometimes they also wish they could leave everything behind, as I would if I knew how. Because, even though I've considered escaping a thousand times, changing scenery, starting somewhere new, something always holds me back. I don't know if it's fear or comfort, but this place remains the only one I know. Is that what's kept me here? Maybe. I don't know. I only know that if I left, it wouldn't be any different. The fear of change, of the unknown, consumes me.

This place doesn't belong to me anymore, but I'm still here. Sometimes I wonder if I'll ever have the strength to leave, to let go of everything tying me down, even if only for a while. But today, like yesterday, I'm still here, because the decisions I want to make feel more terrifying than the ones I've already made. How much longer will I keep repeating this?

Sometimes I think those new people have something I've lost. Maybe you, Future Leo, have already found it. Maybe you, wherever you are, have managed to break free from this routine, leave behind the fears, and live in a way I can't even imagine right now. But if you haven't done it yet, when will you?

With hope,
Present Leo

March 31, 2021

Dear Future Leo,

Today I'm writing to you with a mix of restlessness and determination. I'm not sure if this will make sense to you when you read it, but I needed to get it out of my head. A few days ago, I ran into Erick on the street. It was a strange moment, almost surreal. He was with someone who didn't seem trustworthy, someone with a heavy, dark demeanor. Erick had an expression of anger—or maybe frustration; it looked like he was carrying something far too big to bear. We passed each other for a moment, but neither of us said anything.

I've heard rumors. People always talk, and even though I don't want to believe everything they say, I can't help but think some of it might be true. I don't know what he's caught up in, but it's clearly not good. Seeing him like that left a knot in my stomach. How did we get here? How did someone who was once one of the few people I could talk to turn into a stranger?

But enough about others. I have something important to tell you: I've let it all go. My job, my routine, this city... everything. I'm leaving. I can't stay here anymore, Leo. This place suffocates me, and while I don't know exactly where I'm going, I know I need to start over. I'm going back to my country.

I don't know if this is a brave decision or a cowardly one, but I feel like I have no other choice. This place has taken everything I once cared about. All I have left is the hope that back home, I might find something different, something that gives me the strength to keep going.

I hope that, when you read this, you can look back and understand why I made this decision. Maybe you've even found the peace I'm searching for.

With all the uncertainty in the world,
Leo

Chapter 10. A Return to Familiarity

When I arrived home, my mother greeted me with a long hug, longer than usual. I knew she was holding back tears, but she avoided saying anything emotional right away. While she prepared something to eat in the kitchen, she threw a question my way:

"So, what happened over there? Why did you come back?"

Leaning against the doorframe, I shrugged, trying to sound casual. "I got tired, Mom. I needed a break, and...

well, you know, the snow and cold get exhausting after a while."

She turned slowly, giving me a look that seemed to want to read me entirely. "Is that all?"

I dodged her gaze with a faint smile, wanting to avoid the obvious. "Yeah, Mom. Besides, I missed the food here."

She laughed softly but didn't look entirely convinced. "Well, son, as long as you're here, I want you to rest. But I also hope you get your act together soon. What are you going to do now?"

"I'll figure something out," I replied. My voice sounded sure, but in my mind, everything was as tangled as ever.

The next day, when I visited my dad, the conversation was no less inquisitive.

"So, now what? Weren't you doing well over there?" he asked while pouring two glasses of water at the dining table.

"Yeah, Dad, I just got tired. Everything was routine, and... I don't know, I felt like I needed a change, at least for a while."

He studied me, narrowing his eyes, as if evaluating me. "Are you sure there wasn't something else? Because not long ago, your plans were to come back next year."

“You know how I am; I can’t stay in one place for too long.” I tried to shift the focus with that comment, but he just nodded.

I said goodbye shortly after, and as I walked out the door, I couldn’t shake the feeling that, even though I was back home, I wasn’t at peace with myself.

The first week was strange. All the anxiety I had been carrying for months began to fade little by little, as if simply being here, surrounded by familiar things, had a healing effect. Though I didn’t feel completely settled, there was something comforting about walking the same old streets, the smell of my mom’s morning coffee, and the familiar bustle of the house that never seemed to change.

That afternoon, my phone rang. It was Santiago, one of my closest friends. I hesitated for a moment before answering.

"Leo! What's up, man? When did you get back?" he asked in his usual half-joking, half-surprised tone.

"Yesterday morning. It was all last minute."

"And you didn't say anything? What's up with you? Or are you feeling too European now?"

I laughed, though without much enthusiasm. “Something like that.”

“Well, no way we’re not going out to celebrate. See you at the usual bar. Laura and the others are already in.”

“Okay, fine. What time?”

“Nine. Don’t make it hard—I know you too well.”

I agreed, though part of me doubted if I really wanted to go.

When I got to the bar, everything was the same as always: the loud music, the same worn-out walls, and the same bartender who no longer asked what we wanted to drink. Santiago greeted me with an enthusiastic hug.

"Look who's back, the prodigal son!" he said, laughing.

The others joined in the welcome, full of jokes and comments about how I looked. I sat down, and the conversation flowed, but I felt disconnected, as if I were watching everything from an insurmountable distance.

"So, how was it over there?" Javi asked, raising his beer.

"Good. I learned a lot. Different from this, but good."

"Were you hanging out with European girls or what?" Santiago added with a teasing grin.

"More or less," I replied, forcing a smile to play along.

As they talked about the same topics as always—work, some wild anecdotes, memories from high school—I realized something had changed, but it wasn't the place or them. It was me. Everything I experienced while I was away had left its mark, but here, everything seemed frozen in time.

At the end of the night, Santiago insisted on driving me home. During the ride, he was mostly silent. Then, suddenly,

without taking his eyes off the road, he said:
"Hey, Leo, I don't know what happened over there, but if you need to talk... you know you can count on me, right?"

I looked at him for a moment, trying to figure out if he really wanted to know or if it was just courtesy. "Thanks, Santi. But I'm fine." I lied.

In the days that followed, I repeated the same pattern: outings with my friends, surface-level conversations, but the emptiness remained. No one knew everything I had been through while I was away, and while that gave me a strange sense of relief, it also made me feel more alone than ever.

Weeks passed, and though at first, it seemed like things might improve, that initial sense of relief soon turned into something darker. Each night, the nightmares returned. The image was always the same: the snow, which once reflected light and calm, turned black, as if something inside me were contaminating it. I'd wake up startled, breathing heavily, overwhelmed by a nostalgia so strong it hurt.

During the day, that unease followed me, like a shadow I couldn't ignore. I walked through the familiar streets of my city, but everything felt foreign. The parks where I used to play as a kid, the coffee shops where I spent countless afternoons with friends—they all felt small, faded. Even though I was surrounded by the same people as always, I felt isolated.

One afternoon, while having coffee with Santiago, I tried to express what I'd been feeling.

"Have you started looking for a job here yet? I don't think you'll have a hard time finding one," he commented, stirring his coffee absentmindedly.

"I've tried," I replied after a moment. "But... nothing feels right. It's not the same. Back in the snowy town, at least I felt like I was doing something, even if I didn't love my job."

"Well, of course, things are different here. It's not a tourist town, but that doesn't mean you can't find something you like. You just need to adapt."

His tone was kind, but his words hit me hard. *Adapt.* Was that what I needed to do? I thought about how, despite the challenges, my time there had given me a sense of purpose. Here, everything felt predictable and flat.

That night, I went out for a walk alone. The lights downtown barely illuminated the cracked sidewalks, and the buildings that once seemed impressive now looked worn and forgotten. There was something in the air—a mix of nostalgia and disappointment—that made everything feel more oppressive.

No matter how hard I tried, I couldn't stop comparing this place to the life I had lived there. The cold of the mountains, the long workdays in the snow, the moments of solitude... Somehow, all of it had made me feel more alive. Here, I felt stuck, as though I still had unresolved matters in that town.

The days went by, and while I tried to focus on the present, my mind kept drifting back to the landscapes I had left behind. During a casual conversation with my mother, something sparked within me.

"And that town where you were—was it beautiful? I've heard it's spectacular, but you didn't share much about it..." she asked while putting dishes away in the cupboard.

I nodded. "Yeah, it was. It had massive mountains and lakes that froze in the winter. Sometimes, after work, I'd walk along snow-covered trails just to watch the sunset. But honestly, I never gave myself the time to explore more."

"What a shame. You're always saying you want to travel and see new places, but when you get the chance, you don't take advantage of it."

I didn't respond, but her words stayed with me for the rest of the day. She was right. I had been surrounded by stunning landscapes, places any tourist would dream of visiting, but I was always too tired or too distracted by work to appreciate them. I never hiked to the top of a mountain, never visited the forests in spring, never tried skiing like everyone else there seemed to enjoy. Even the little local restaurants went unnoticed by me.

That night, lying in bed, my mind started to fill in the gaps with images: the snow-covered town, the familiar faces at work, the winding trails lined with pine trees. It felt like I had left something unfinished.

What if I go back, but this time I do it differently? I thought. Maybe it was a way to reconcile everything that had happened, to give myself a second chance—not just with the place, but with myself. If I returned, I didn't want to fall into the same routines. This time, I promised myself, I would explore. I'd walk the mountain trails, find the hidden spots I had ignored, and learn to enjoy the silence and the cold.

The idea started as a seed, but by the next morning, it had grown into a plan. I didn't know how long I would stay or exactly what I would do, but I knew I couldn't remain here. Something in me needed to go back. Maybe this time, I could find something more—or perhaps confront my old ghosts.

The following morning, after firmly deciding to return, I began packing my things. It wasn't much, but the process felt different this time. There was a renewed energy, a kind of excitement I hadn't felt in a long time. When I went down to the dining room, my mom was making breakfast.

"Awake so early?" she said, surprised.

"I'm going back."

She stopped stirring her coffee and looked at me intently. "Back where?"

"To the town. I want to save some money again, but this time I'm going with a fresh mindset, ready to do things differently."

A small, warm smile formed on her face. "I'm glad to see you so determined. I think you needed this time here to figure out what you wanted."

"Yeah... something like that." I took a sip of my coffee while looking out the window. "This time feels different. I want to explore more, really get to know the place. I want to do more than just work."

My mom nodded. "I always thought that place changed you—for the better. Just take care of yourself, okay?"

The conversation left me with a sense of relief. Even though she didn't say it outright, she seemed genuinely happy to see me with a clear purpose. We finished breakfast while discussing what I would need for the trip.

After a few quick goodbyes—including a hurried hug from Santiago and some last-minute advice from my parents—I caught my flight the next day. The journey gave me time to think, but also to imagine what it would be like to return. This time, I wasn't running away or desperately searching for answers; I was going with the intention of living something new in a place I already knew.

When I arrived at the airport, everything felt more familiar, as if I had never really left. I hailed a taxi to take me to the town, but just before getting in, the driver rushed off to the bathroom, leaving me to juggle my luggage in the freezing wind. Another taxi sped by, splashing my pants with dirty water from a puddle.

I looked down at the dark stain covering half my leg. A couple of months ago, this would've been enough to ruin my day. But instead of getting angry, I let out an unexpected laugh. *Welcome back,* I thought.

Once in the taxi, as I watched the snowy mountains draw closer in the distance, I felt I had made the right decision. This return wasn't about going back to the past—it was about building something new. And for the first time in a long while, I felt excited about what was to come.

The same jobs quickly rehired me. This time, however, I set a condition: I would work fewer hours. Of course, it was still more than the average person, but now I had enough time to explore new activities and do more than just save money.

And so, I did. I started skiing. I wasn't exactly good at it; my first attempts were a disaster of constant falls and clumsy turns. But I had fun. I also dared to try other things, small activities I would have never considered before. It was true I was saving less, but for the first time in a long while, I felt like I was truly living my life.

One morning, while skiing and falling just as often as I advanced, something caught my attention. A few meters away, a girl lost control and, at full speed, crashed directly into a tree. At first, I found it funny; something about the clumsy way it happened made me smile. But that smile disappeared in seconds.

The girl wasn't moving. Several rescuers arrived quickly, sliding down with precision and professionalism. The scene, which initially seemed like just another joke on the slopes, turned into something entirely different. I sat on the snow, watching as they lifted her onto a stretcher and carried her away. I couldn't take my eyes off the spot where she had hit.

When I got a bit closer, I saw a small bloodstain left in the snow. Bright red, it stood out vividly against the immense white. A chill ran down my spine. There was something almost symbolic about that image, something that reminded me of the tragedy that had marked my life not long ago.

Yet, at the same time, something within me surprised me. The memory was still there, but it felt vaguer, less sharp. I looked at the snow, the blood, the tree. And while the echo of that tragedy still lingered, this time it didn't feel like it was consuming me. I stayed there a moment longer, letting the cold wind brush against my face. Then I stood up and moved on.

Chapter 11. To the Summit

The more balanced rhythm of my life at that moment kept me energized, filled with a sense of purpose I hadn't experienced in a long time. But I still felt the need to push further, to try something I had never done before. That's when I decided to climb a mountain.

I started researching and discovered that, in the world of mountaineering, mountains are classified according to their level of difficulty—at least in the area where I was living. They range from 1 to 5, with the first being practically a simple hike and the last an extreme challenge reserved for the most experienced climbers.

Since I'm brave but also a bit reckless, I told myself: "I'm not so useless as to pick a level 1, but I'm not suicidal enough to attempt a level 5. Something in the middle sounds perfect."

So, I chose a level 3 mountain. It wasn't the wisest choice for a beginner, but as often happens, enthusiasm outweighed caution. I bought the necessary gear: proper boots, thermal clothing, a headlamp, and a backpack with essentials. I watched some videos to prepare, though nothing could really anticipate what I was about to experience.

The day finally arrived. I began my ascent at 2:00 a.m., aiming to reach the summit just in time for sunrise, which would be at 7:20 a.m. I had five hours to make it. In theory, it seemed like enough.

The cold was biting, even with all the layers I wore. Every sip of the hot coffee I had prepared before leaving was a small boost that helped me keep moving. The headlamp lit the path ahead, but the darkness surrounding me seemed endless. It was as if the rest of the world didn't exist, as if I were completely alone in an icy abyss.

What no one tells you in the tutorials is how unsettling it can be to walk in the dark, surrounded by sounds you can't identify. The crunch of snow under your boots, the whisper of the wind, and those mysterious noises in the distance that could be anything—from moving branches to a mountain lion. Every few steps, I stopped, shone the lamp in all directions, and made sure nothing was following me.

The fear was there, always present, but something about it drove me forward. A mix of adrenaline and determination told me I had to keep going. Time passed slowly, and though my body was already starting to feel the effort, the promise of a sunrise at the summit was enough to keep me moving.

As the slope became steeper, I began to understand why mountains have such specific classifications. What initially seemed like a challenging but manageable hike had turned into a battle against my own body. Each step was heavier than the last, each breath harder to catch.

The snow didn't completely cover the path, but rocky sections began to appear more frequently. My pace slowed, and I increasingly relied on my hands to keep my balance. Fortunately, within my recklessness, I had the luck to choose a favorable day: it hadn't snowed in the past two weeks, and the temperatures, though freezing, were mild for a place like this.

The snow season was coming to an end, and that played in my favor. The previous weeks had allowed some sections of the trail to clear, making the trek less slippery. But that didn't eliminate the exhaustion.

Suffering but determined, I kept going. The sky was starting to lighten; the dark tones of dawn slowly gave way to the pale blue of an imminent sunrise.

I looked at my watch and knew I wouldn't reach the summit before the sun rose. For a moment, I felt disappointment, but I decided to keep climbing. Even if I didn't reach the summit at the time I had hoped, the simple fact of being here, attempting something so new and challenging, was enough to keep me going.

With every step, I silently repeated to myself: “Keep going. Just a little more.”

I climbed a few meters and then had to stop. My legs were trembling, and though I was breathing deeply, I felt like my lungs couldn’t take in all the oxygen they needed. The slope and the altitude were taking their toll, but I kept telling myself over and over that I could do it.

The moment of sunrise arrived. I stopped on a rock that seemed stable, pulled a small snack from my backpack, and took a few minutes to appreciate what lay before me. “How beautiful the world can be.” The colors unfolding on the horizon were a spectacle: shades of orange and pink mixed with the blues and grays of the sky. A few clouds drifted slowly, as if floating there solely to decorate the scene. The nearby mountains were bathed in that warm light that seemed to illuminate even the darkest corners of the soul.

It's incredible how, in these moments, physical pain seems to vanish just by looking at something so sublime.

After taking a deep breath and exhaling in a way that made me feel a little lighter, I prepared to continue. My steps were slow but steady. The sun was beginning to rise, its rays slipping through the clouds and lightly warming my face. I felt grateful for the weather, for this experience, even for how exhausted I was.

But as I was just a few dozen meters from the summit, I felt a terrible pull in my right leg. An unbearable cramp brought me to the ground. I let out a groan and tried to stretch my leg carefully, but the pain wouldn't subside. For a moment, I thought about giving up and turning back. "Is this a sign? Should I stop here?"

I took a deep breath and waited. Ten long minutes passed before the cramp began to ease. I massaged my leg while telling myself, "I didn't come all this way to give up now." Slowly and carefully, I got back on my feet. The summit was close, and I wasn't going to let one more obstacle stop me.

Finally, I made it. I reached the summit. All the surrounding mountains were covered with a delicate blanket of snow, as if someone had sprinkled powdered sugar over them.

The lakes hidden among the peaks reflected a sky still partially clear, and the vastness of the landscape was overwhelming. I was left speechless. I had climbed a relatively small mountain, just over 15,000 feet, but the euphoria I felt was as if I had conquered Everest.

I stayed there for at least an hour, taking in the view, letting the scenery fill me with energy. I took out a small snack I had prepared and enjoyed it as if it were a feast. With every bite, I looked around, imprinting every detail in my mind. The wind, which until then had been a whisper, began to blow more strongly. It was as if the mountain itself was announcing that it was time to leave.

The wind stirred up the snow on the ground like dust in a desert, creating swirling patterns that danced at will. I knew I shouldn't stay much longer. So I stood up, secured my backpack, and began the descent carefully.

As I descended, the wind continued to grow stronger, striking my face like tiny needles of ice. The sky, which had been my ally throughout the climb, began to darken. Black clouds moved quickly, covering the sun and bringing with them a sense of urgency.

This wasn't part of the plan, I thought, feeling a knot in my stomach. I quickened my pace, knowing that conditions on the mountain could change in a matter of minutes. Every time I looked up, the sky seemed more threatening, as if it wanted to remind me that, while beautiful, nature can also be unforgiving.

At least I managed to make it halfway down the mountain when a snowstorm hit. The wind howled fiercely, and the snow fell so densely that I could barely see a few meters ahead. My heart began to pound as one thought repeated in my mind: How could I forget to check the weather today? I had checked the forecast a few days earlier, but, like any novice, I had neglected to do so on the same day.

The cold seeped through every corner of my clothing, and the noise of the wind made everything feel even more intimidating. As I struggled to move forward, I came across a small gap between two rocks that offered some protection. Without hesitation, I took shelter there, determined to wait out the storm.

The minutes stretched on like hours. Sitting in that tiny space, fear was my only companion. I tried to distract myself by thinking about the warmth of home or what I would eat when I got back, but the storm felt endless. It lasted about 30 minutes, though to me, it felt like a small eternity.

Finally, the wind began to calm, and the snow stopped falling so heavily. Now, only a few flakes drifted down, almost gently, as if the mountain had decided to grant me a reprieve. Still shivering, I stepped out of my makeshift shelter, adjusted my backpack, and took a deep breath. It was time to continue the descent.

Now I had a small problem. Which way should I go? The storm had completely erased the packed snow trail that had marked my ascent. Around me, everything looked peaceful, even beautiful, but the reality was different. It was as if the mountain were mocking me. "And now what will you do?" I thought, as if nature itself were challenging me.

With no other options, I had to rely on my intuition. I looked around, searching for anything, any feature that seemed familiar, but there wasn't much to recognize. When I climbed up, everything had been dark, and my focus had been more on my steps than on my surroundings. The only thing I could do now was orient myself by the slight terrain relief and move forward cautiously.

I walked a few meters, stopping now and then to observe. I tried to recall if that rock or that group of trees looked familiar, but everything seemed the same, covered by a uniform layer of fresh snow. It was a frustrating, almost ironic situation. I had reached the summit and faced a storm, but what unsettled me the most was the uncertainty of not knowing if I was truly descending on the right side of the mountain.

The hours passed, and I kept descending. My biggest fear was not being able to find the start of the trail. I knew that once I located it, I could easily reach the bus station that would take me back home. But now, lost among trees and untouched snow, everything felt as distant as it was unlikely.

The sun was beginning to set, casting long shadows across the mountain.

There were no clear markers, and I increasingly found myself surrounded by trees I didn't recall seeing during my ascent. The cold grew more intense with each passing minute, and the idea of having to spend the night on the mountain was starting to feel like a real possibility. *How prepared am I for something like this?* I wondered as I tightened my jacket and wiggled my fingers inside my gloves to keep the blood flowing.

Midway through my improvised descent, I came across a section of ground covered by a thin, slippery layer of ice. I tried to move carefully, but as soon as I took a step, my foot slipped, and I fell backward, sliding about five meters downhill. Luckily, I stopped before hitting a tree, but my backpack got caught on a branch, and I had to struggle to retrieve it. What if I hadn't been so lucky? I thought, my heart racing.

Eventually, I recovered my backpack and continued, more alert than before. But just a few minutes later, I heard a sound that made my stomach drop: a cracking noise. I looked down and saw the layer of snow beneath me starting to fracture. Before I could react, the ground gave way, and I fell down a small drop, hitting my side against a rock. The pain was sharp, but at least nothing seemed broken.

I lay there for a few moments, breathing heavily as I tried to assess my situation.

Looking up, I saw that I had fallen into the bed of a small frozen stream. The water, though scarce, flowed beneath the layer of ice. If this area melts frequently, it must lead to a valley or something similar, I thought, clinging to any idea that could guide me back to the trail.

With effort, I got up and began following the stream, stumbling and staggering over the uneven terrain. Daylight was almost completely gone when, rounding a corner, I finally saw something that made me smile: footprints. They weren't mine, but they were fresh and seemed to be heading in the right direction.

With renewed hope, I followed the footprints, which eventually led me to a spot I recognized from my ascent. I was finally back on the trail. Despite the extreme exhaustion and the pain in my side, I managed to reach the bus station just as the last bus of the day was about to depart.

As I sat on the bus and looked out the window, I felt a mix of relief, exhaustion, and strange pride. I had made many mistakes, but I had survived. I didn't know if I would ever attempt something like that again, but for now, all I wanted was a hot shower and my bed. Suddenly, everything went black.

Chapter 12. The darkness inside

I appeared on a street that seemed like a blend between my hometown and the one I had started calling home, wrapped in a thick fog. Suddenly, a light turned on above me, slowly illuminating everything around. I felt drawn to familiar noises, as if someone was calling me. I followed the sounds to an old house—the one where I grew up. Everyone was there, even my parents, who had been separated but were acting here as if everything was fine, as if they'd never been apart.

“Good to see you, son,” my mother said, smiling as she used to.

“We’ve been waiting for you,” my father added, as though nothing had ever changed.

I sat with them, surrounded by faces I loved. My grandmother, who had passed away, was also there, serving food with her warm smile. Everything felt so perfect, like a scene plucked from another time.

“Everything alright, Grandma?” I asked, eating and savoring the moment.

“I’m glad to see you at peace,” she said, looking at me intently.

The conversation started normal at first. Everyone seemed happy to see me, and even the arguments that used to arise in real life were absent. But soon, something shifted. My mother stared at me, her smile slowly fading.

“What did you do, Leo?” she asked in a tone I didn’t recognize.

The atmosphere grew tense. The others, who had been smiling, began to look at me too, their expressions changing. They all stared, and something in their gazes chilled me to the bone.

“What did you do?” my mother repeated, now more firmly. “Did you really think you could escape everything you left behind?”

My father spoke too, his voice now heavy with disapproval. "You can't just run away, Leo. You have to face it."

My cousins and uncles, who had been silently watching, also started questioning me, all with serious, accusing expressions. "We knew," one of them said. "You couldn't hide forever. You're a liar."

I felt trapped, as though my entire life was unraveling at that moment. The house no longer felt welcoming, and the fog began creeping in, clouding my mind and my ability to understand what was happening. Nobody was looking at me with kindness, nobody was understanding me. They all wanted answers, but I didn't know what to say. The warmth I had felt at first had disappeared, leaving only a deep void. What had I done? Why were they all looking at me like this? Confusion overwhelmed me, but I couldn't escape the silent accusations that hung over me.

Everything went dark, as if the house and its inhabitants had vanished in an instant. The silence was so oppressive it felt like it could crush me. Then, out of nowhere, a light flickered on above me. Its beam was cold and weak, barely illuminating a few meters around me. I was no longer in my childhood home; now I seemed to be in the middle of a snowy forest, with the shadows of the trees stretching into infinity. The snow beneath my feet made a faint crunch with every step, like walking on glass.

The cold was palpable, as though the darkness itself was alive and breathing ice. A dense mist crept among the trees, moving with an almost human purpose. That's when I saw it: a figure emerging from the shadows.

As it came closer, I recognized the face. It was Erick... but something was horribly wrong with him. He had a hole in his forehead, right in the center, its edges blackened as if time itself had tried to close it in vain. His skin was pale, almost translucent, and his eyes, though empty, seemed filled with something indescribable—a mix of sorrow and reproach.

"You're not going to help me either, are you?" Erick said, his voice sounding like the echo of a distant scream, raspy and heavy with regret.

I couldn't move. I tried to respond, but no words came out of my mouth, as if something invisible was gripping my throat. Erick took another step toward me, and each time he did, the snow around him turned red. I looked down and saw that I, too, was leaving crimson footprints behind me, as though something was draining life from us both.

"Are you just going to keep running?" he continued, his voice now louder, almost accusing. “First her, and now… me. Always looking the other way.”

I wanted to scream that it wasn’t true, that I didn’t know what he was talking about, but the weight of his gaze crushed me. In his eyes, I saw something unbearably familiar: it was as if I was looking at my own reflection in a distorted mirror.

Suddenly, the forest began to change. The trees turned into columns of rusted iron, and the snow transformed into murky water rising rapidly, as if trying to drown me. Erick was now closer, his face inches from mine, his icy breath forming words I couldn’t understand. Behind him, a crowd of shadows began to appear, their faces blurred, all staring at me. Each one repeated in an unsettling murmur, "Will you lie to us too?"

I tried to run, but my legs wouldn't move. Everything turned to chaos. The iron columns began collapsing around me, and the snow, now a swirling mass of freezing water, rose to my chest. Erick faded into the mist, but his voice lingered in the air, repeating over and over: "You're not going to help me either?"

Then everything when dark again. Just darkness and silence.

When I woke up suddenly, I wasn't in my bed. The white ceiling and the flickering fluorescent lights, buzzing faintly, made me blink several times before I could process where I was. The smell of disinfectant and the distant sound of a heart monitor confirmed what took me a few seconds to realize: I was in a hospital.

I tried to move, but a sharp pain shot through my head, like a hot knife buried in my skull. Instinctively, I reached for my forehead, but I found a thick bandage covering part of it. My mouth was dry, and when I tried to speak, only a raspy whisper came out.

“What happened?”

A nurse, who had been writing something on a tablet at the foot of my bed, looked up and quickly approached me.

"You're finally awake. You've been unconscious for several hours," she said with a mix of professionalism and concern.

"Where am I?" I managed to ask more clearly, though my voice still sounded weak.

"You're in the county hospital. You suffered a seizure and lost consciousness. It seems to have been caused by a concussion."

I frowned, trying to remember. My mind was a whirlwind of fragmented images. Erick's words echoed in my head, but I couldn't pinpoint the exact moment when everything fell apart.

"How did I get here?" I asked, though I feared the answer.

"The ambulance brought you. According to the paramedics, you collapsed while you were on a bus. They said you fell and hit your head—you had some bleeding on your scalp."

I tried to piece it together, but everything was blurry. The last thing I clearly remembered was Erick's face in my thoughts, his words echoing like a haunting refrain: *"You're not going to help me either?"* After that, only darkness.

"A concussion?" I repeated, as if saying it aloud would help me absorb it better.

The nurse nodded. "We had to do a CT scan. Fortunately, there's no severe hematoma, but your brain is swollen. That's what caused the seizure. You'll need to stay under observation."

I closed my eyes, trying to calm the flood of emotions overwhelming me. Each time I tried to focus, the images from the dream came back stronger: Erick in the snowy forest, with that empty gaze, and the blood slowly seeping from his head. The detail of the wound was so vivid that it churned my stomach.

"Am I... in danger?" I asked, dreading the answer.

"For now, you're stable, but you need to rest. The swelling could worsen if you don't follow the doctor's instructions. And you should try to avoid stress—anything that causes you anxiety could be a trigger."

Avoid stress. It was an ironic recommendation, considering that every part of me was caught in a web of confusion, guilt, and fear. I tried to sit up, but the pain in my head made me stop.

"Can I make a call?" I asked, feeling an urgent need to contact someone, though I wasn't sure who.

"Of course, but not right now. We need you to rest first," the nurse said while adjusting something on the monitor.

I nodded weakly, though I knew I wouldn't be able to sleep. Erick's words kept echoing in my mind, and now, combined with the experience of waking up in a hospital, they left me with an unsettling sense that something beyond my understanding was unfolding.

"Was anyone with me when I was brought in?" I asked before the nurse walked away.

She shook her head. "No, just you. The paramedics said someone on the bus called for help, but they didn't leave their name. Why? Were you meeting someone?"

I didn't answer. Erick's face materialized once again in my mind, like a specter I couldn't exorcize. I didn't know if he was connected to what had happened, but one thing was clear: this wasn't the end of something—it was the beginning.

Chapter 13. If You Don't Face Your Lies, They'll Face You

A few days later, I was discharged. I decided not to tell anyone; I didn't want to worry them more than necessary. I only contacted work because I couldn't afford to lose my job. I told them about the accident but downplayed many details. I didn't mention the seizure or the fact that I had woken up in a hospital with no memory of how I got there.

"The doctor said with a week of rest and a final checkup, I'll be fine," I explained over the phone, making sure to sound relaxed. In reality, I had decided to take at least two weeks off. I needed more time—not just for my body to recover but also to try to sort out my thoughts.

At first, the days passed in a kind of haze. The persistent headache worsened whenever I tried to think about what had happened, as if my own body was forcing me to avoid it. So I gave in. I let time slip by, watching TV without really paying attention, eating without appetite, and trying to sleep even though the nights were long and restless.

“This can’t last forever,” I thought one morning as I stared at my bedroom ceiling. Rays of sunlight streamed through the window, illuminating specks of dust in the air. A week had passed since I was discharged from the hospital, and although the headache had lessened, the echo of that dream and Erick's words continued to haunt me.

I took a deep breath, picked up my phone, and stared at it for a moment, hesitating. I knew I couldn't avoid this any longer. If there was one thing I had learned in those days, it was that silence and distance had done nothing to calm my mind. It was time to face whatever was happening.

I dialed Erick's number, feeling like each ring of the phone matched the pounding of my heart.

"Come on, pick up..." I murmured to myself as my pulse quickened.

The call went to voicemail. I closed my eyes and ran a hand through my hair, frustrated. Now what?

For a moment, I considered leaving a message, but something stopped me. I wasn't sure what to say or how to approach the subject. Instead, I opened the messaging app and quickly typed:

"Erick, it's me. We need to talk. Let me know when you're free."

I sent it before I could change my mind and set the phone aside. All I could do now was wait, though the waiting felt unbearable.

The next day, when morning came, I grabbed my phone, determined, and wrote another message:
"Erick, how are you? Let's catch up." I hit send and stared at the screen, but no response came.

I decided to give it some time. I made myself a cup of coffee and tried to distract myself, but the thought that something might be wrong with him wouldn't leave me. A few hours later, I tried again:
"Hey, Erick, just want to make sure you're okay. Call me when you can."

Days passed. Nothing. Erick's silence was beginning to weigh on me more than I wanted to admit.

I lay on the couch, holding my phone in my hand, and sent another message: "Everything okay, bro? Let me know if you need anything."

As I waited, my thoughts piled up. *What could be happening? Why isn't he responding?* I had distanced myself from Erick a bit after what happened with Brooke, not intentionally, but because things had changed. *Is he upset because I pulled away?* I wondered. Although it seemed hard to believe, I couldn't rule it out.

Taking a deep breath, I picked up the phone and decided to call him again. The phone rang several times, but it went to voicemail once more. "This is getting too strange... What is Erick thinking? Why doesn't he want to talk to me?"

A knot began to form in my stomach. *Maybe he's dealing with something bigger than I imagined. Or maybe... did he hear something that upset him?* I tried to make sense of it, but every answer I came up with opened new questions.

Finally, I set the phone aside, frustrated. That dream continued to haunt me; the lingering sense of guilt was something I couldn't fully explain. Something was wrong, and all I could do was wait and keep trying.

Another day passed, one of those days when you don't expect much and just want to go home to rest. I was walking through the park, feeling the cool air moving through the trees, when suddenly, in the distance, I saw Erick. He was sitting on a bench, his head bowed, as if lost in thought. At first, I hesitated. I didn't know if I should approach him. Weeks had passed, and I had tried to contact Erick several times without success.

But something inside me said this was my chance. Without overthinking it, I walked toward him with a determined stride, trying to ignore the knot in my stomach.

"Erick!" I called out cheerfully, not caring if anyone else heard. Erick immediately looked up, and for a moment, I thought my friend would respond with a smile, like he always used to. But when I saw the expression on his face, my excitement faded.

Erick didn't smile. He didn't show any of the surprise you'd expect when bumping into an old friend. He simply stared at me with an emotionless expression, almost one of disdain.

"What are you doing here?" were the first words Erick said, his voice tense, as if seeing me was the last thing he wanted at that moment. I stopped a step away from the bench, feeling a strange pressure in the air.

"I just wanted to see how you were," I said in a softer, more cautious tone. "It's been a while since I've heard from you. I thought we could catch up... How have you been?"

Erick stood up from the bench slowly, never taking his eyes off me. The tension between us was palpable, like a knife that could slice through the air.
"I don't want to talk," he said, his words clear but cold, like an invisible wall rising between us.

"Erick, come on, what's going on?" I insisted, worried, unable to understand why my friend seemed so distant, so different. "You can't just disappear. Why haven't you responded to me? I want to help; you know you can count on me."

That's when Erick took a step closer, his eyes narrowing, and said, with barely contained anger:
"I know everything!"
I froze, unable to process what I was hearing.
"What? What are you talking about?" I asked, confused and alarmed, unsure of what to expect from my friend. Erick took a deep breath, as if trying to calm himself before dropping what seemed like a bomb.

"I know, Leo. I know Brooke wasn't just your friend," he said, his voice tense and full of resentment. I felt my legs weaken, and a chill ran down my spine. I didn't understand. What was Erick saying?

"What?" I murmured, my voice barely audible.
"What are you insinuating?"

"Someone told me that months before everything happened, they saw you with Brooke. You two were holding hands," Erick said, his words landing like stones. The shock left me breathless.

I swallowed hard, trying to process the information.
"Who told you that? Who lied to you?" I asked, desperate for an explanation.
"That's not how it happened, Erick. It's not what you think."

Erick frowned, his expression shifting from anger to disdain.

"A coworker," he said, as if that was proof enough. "And you never told me the truth, Leo. What else should I know?"

I took a step back, feeling the air around me grow heavy.

"It wasn't like that," I repeated, almost pleading, though I wasn't sure if Erick was really listening. How could he be so certain of something I didn't even fully understand myself? My relationship with Brooke had been complicated, something that had ended long ago. How could Erick have misunderstood everything so completely?

But he didn't listen. With a sharp turn, he began walking away, as if he didn't want to waste another second on a conversation he no longer cared about.

“Whatever you say... after this, I wouldn’t be surprised if she killed herself because of you,” he muttered without looking back, before quickly leaving, leaving me standing there alone, overwhelmed by a silence that now felt suffocating.

I stood there, unable to react, as confusion and helplessness consumed me. What had really happened between Brooke and me? Was it my fault? How far did Erick’s assumptions go about what I had supposedly caused?

All this time, I had avoided the subject. I had kept the truth to myself, hoping it would never come to light. Not because I felt guilty, but because I didn't want anyone to think I had broken Brooke's heart or contributed to her tragic decision. But my silence had created exactly what I had tried to avoid: the appearance of guilt. By trying to protect myself, I had fueled the suspicions that now haunted me.

Chapter 14. The Night We Met

One day before being "introduced" at that bar by Erick, Leo and Brooke had what would be their last "date." It wasn't the typical dramatic farewell, but rather a calm and honest conversation where they both shared their most sincere feelings.

They were sitting in a small café, the atmosphere relaxed and almost empty, as if the world had set the stage for an unpressured chat. Leo, sensing something wasn't quite right, was the first to break the silence.

"I think you already know this, but I'm not looking for anything serious. Not right now, at least," he said softly, watching Brooke idly play with her coffee cup.

Brooke looked up, not surprised but rather relieved.

"I hadn't said it, but neither am I. I've been trying to figure out what I want, and honestly, I don't think this is the time for anything more. And I don't want us to complicate things," she replied, and Leo saw in her eyes an understanding that could only come from being on the same page.

They both laughed softly, relieved not to have to pretend their feelings were something deeper.

"I think we're on the same wavelength," Brooke said.

"I don't think we're meant to be more than friends. And I'm okay with that because I know you'd make a great friend."

"I feel the same," Leo said with a genuine smile.
"And honestly, I think it's better this way. There's no point in forcing something that doesn't have that spark, right?"

"Exactly," she replied.
"Sometimes friendship is the most real thing. And that, at least, is something I know won't fade easily. Besides, these past few weeks have been fun."

The conversation flowed effortlessly, like a river finding its path without obstacles. While they realized the "magic" that might have existed between them wasn't there, they understood that the connection they shared was unique in its own way. It was a quiet kind of magic, uncomplicated, the kind that reassures you someone will be a good friend, no matter what.

At the end of their last outing, Leo and Brooke's conversation was relaxed and pressure-free. They knew what they wanted: to be friends. There was no room for games or illusions anymore.

"Hey, but I'll see you tomorrow, right? You're the new guy at work..." Brooke asked with a light smile as she adjusted her coat.

"Yeah, thanks for helping me get the interview. It'll be interesting working with you, though no one needs to know about our story. I don't want people bothering us at work," Leo responded.

"Well, besides, who knows? Maybe we'll end up being great friends in this new chapter," Brooke said, half-joking, half-serious, with a knowing smile.

Leo looked at her and, sensing it was the right moment, replied sincerely, "Maybe. I think we have enough in common for at least that to work."

They looked at each other for a few seconds. The tension faded away, and no more words were needed. They said goodbye with a smile, understanding that, in this case, simplicity was the best choice: a genuine, uncomplicated friendship.

It's true. We knew each other before, from a party where everything started with jokes and flirting. The day Erick "introduced" us, we pretended not to know each other. There was no need for a detailed plan; it was as if we had both instantly decided how to act: a chance to restart, to build something different, something right.

Brooke and I had a connection, but not the kind that turns into a future. We had our outings, our moments, and then, on a quiet night, we decided to be honest. We weren't compatible, but we could be something simpler, something purer.

Friends. There were no tears, no drama, just an unspoken agreement that what we had shared was better left as a fleeting memory.

Sometimes I tell myself that everything that happened afterward had nothing to do with me. Her problems were hers, and I was just a brief, almost irrelevant chapter in her story. But then I think of Erick, of the look of disbelief and anger on his face when he found out. How he looked at me, as if I had betrayed something sacred. I never told him about it, not because I felt guilty, but because it had been a pact between Brooke and me. No one else needed to know.

But maybe... maybe that's just the story I tell myself to be able to sleep at night. A narrative that absolves me of guilt, that makes me the loyal friend and the innocent man. Perhaps there's another story buried deep down, one I don't want to face. Something that will remain hidden, just like the secret we swore to keep.

It will never be known, and I don't care if it is.

Chapter 15. A Proper Goodbye

One afternoon, while walking calmly by the river, I heard someone call out to me.

"Hey, man! Hey!"

A guy approached quickly. At first, I didn't recognize him.

"Do you remember me?" he said with a wide, eager smile.

I pretended I did, not wanting to make him feel awkward. "Of course! How've you been?" I responded with fake cheer while desperately trying to dig through my memory for his name.

"It's been a while," he said, and then he added something that left me frozen. "Hey, thanks for giving Brooke the little box. She never called me back or replied to any messages, so I guess she didn't like it," he said, laughing nervously. "Although, I haven't seen her in a while... How's she doing? I'm Chris, remember?"

I froze, trying to process what I had just heard. Now I remembered. Before leaving the city, Chris had asked me to give something to Brooke—a small box whose existence I had long buried in my memory. By the time he returned, the news of her death had likely faded, like everything else about her. She wasn't particularly well-known in town, and the box... I didn't even remember where I had left it.

"Uh... yeah, sure, man. You know how Brooke was; she wasn't big on details," I lied, though I didn't know why.

Chris seemed to accept the answer, though with some resignation on his face. "Well... at least I tried. But, how is she doing?" His expression shifted to genuine curiosity.

"She decided to get a fresh start," I improvised, feeling the knot in my throat tighten with every word. "She moved somewhere that made her happier, I suppose..."

"Well, I'm glad for her. And good seeing you again. Take care, man."

"Sure, see you," I replied, watching as he walked away with that kind, unassuming smile.

I stood by the river, my mind blank and my heart racing. **What madness...** I thought as the weight of everything came crashing down on me.

Wasting no time, I hurried home. I knew that box was somewhere, and for the first time in a long time, I felt an urgent need to find it.

I searched the entire house, opening drawers, checking shelves, and exploring forgotten corners. With every step, my frustration grew, as if the universe itself was determined to hide what I needed to find. Finally, upon entering the closet and pulling an old coat, something fell to the floor with a dull thud. I stood still for a moment, staring at the small box that had rolled to my feet.

As I crouched to pick it up, the lid slid open, revealing its contents. A necklace came into view: a small snowflake with a black diamond at its center, surrounded by tiny diamonds on each branch and golden accents. I held it in my hands, examining every detail with a mix of awe and confusion. **Why did I never wonder what was in this box?** I thought, feeling a pang of guilt settle deep in my chest.

The necklace shimmered under the dim light of my room, each glint seeming to remind me of the weight of what I had let slip by. I sat on the edge of my bed, the necklace still in my hands. I didn't know what to think or do. All of this, everything it represented, felt like a puzzle I had chosen to ignore for far too long.

The next morning, I got up early, determined to do something that, although late, felt like it needed to be done. I carefully placed the necklace back into the box, closing it with a sort of silent reverence. Then, I tucked it into the pocket of my coat and headed for the overlook.

The path there was quiet, almost deserted, with the morning chill biting at my cheeks. In the distance, the mountains were draped in a light veil of mist, and the nearby river mirrored the gray sky. I arrived at the overlook just as the sun began to break through the clouds, casting faint rays of light across the landscape.

This place was special. It was where Brooke and I had one of our deepest conversations, about death and what might come after.

I found a secluded corner, a spot with the perfect view of the valley, and knelt on the ground. The soil was hard from the cold, but slowly, I managed to dig a small hole. Before placing the box inside, I pulled out a small letter I had written the night before. I carefully rolled it up and placed it alongside the necklace in the box. I closed the lid gently, nestled it in the hole, and began to cover it with soil.

When I finished, I stayed there for a while, staring at the spot where I had buried it. I didn't say anything out loud; I wasn't sure if that made sense, but in my mind, everything was clear. This was my goodbye, however belated. Something I hadn't been able to give her before.

When they found her that day, there was no time to process anything. Her brother took her body back to his city. I didn't attend the funeral. There was no way he would have welcomed me after what he had said to all of us. But here, in this corner we had shared, I felt like I could say goodbye in my own way.

I stood up slowly, brushing the dirt from my hands, and looked at the horizon one last time. I hope this, somehow, reaches you, I thought before turning and starting the walk back home.

Dear Brooke,

I never thought writing this letter would be so hard, and at the same time, so necessary. It took me far too long to confront what I truly feel, to acknowledge how much your absence hurts. I pretended to be strong, hid behind indifference, as if that could make the wound disappear. But it didn't work. Nothing does.

I want to say I'm sorry. Sorry for not being the friend you needed, for not hearing the things you couldn't say out loud. Sorry for being so close, yet so far, when you needed me the most. I'm sorry with all my heart, Brooke. If I could turn back time, I would do things differently.

It's heartbreaking to think about how we leave impressions of ourselves on the people we meet. To Erick, you were the girl we all let fall. To your brother, you were a victim of our blindness and silence. To others, you were just a broken girl who faded away. But to me, Brooke, you will always be one of the most complex and brilliant souls I've ever known.

To be honest, at first, I was angry with you. I felt betrayed, confused. I went so far as to delete all your photos, to try and erase every trace of you, as if that could ease the anger I felt. It wasn't fair to you, I know, but I can't lie to you: it hurt so much that the only thing I could do was blame you. I was angry because, though it sounds unempathetic, you also let yourself fall. There were so many different things you could have done, so many doors you could have opened. But over time, I understood it wasn't that simple—that the weight you carried was far more than any of us could have imagined.

There's so much I want to say to you, but words will never be enough. Sometimes I wonder if you ever knew how much I valued you, how much you meant to me. Now, that question haunts me. It hurts that this is my goodbye, that the only thing I can do is write these words and leave them here, where we once shared our deepest conversations.

You know what kills me? That I couldn't say goodbye to you. I wasn't there when you left. I wasn't there to hold you, to tell you things could get better, that you weren't alone. And now, all I have left is this letter and a void I will never be able to fill.

I hope, with everything in me, that there's something after this—a place, a space, a time where I can find you again. A place where we can talk, where I can say all of this to you while looking into your eyes. Because if there's one thing I want more than anything, it's the chance to mend what was broken.

For now, all I can do is leave this letter with you and hope that, in some way, you feel how deeply sorry I am for failing you. Brooke, the fragment of you that I carry with me, I lay it to rest here, in this place that will always be yours, though I will never stop carrying you in my heart.

I will always love you,
I will always remember you.
With all my heart,
Leo.

www.ingramcontent.com/pod-product-compliance
Lightning Source LLC
Chambersburg PA
CBHW051041250726
48656CB00001B/91

* 9 7 9 8 3 0 5 2 5 4 5 0 1 *